Biblioteca
Aeronáutica
aviación en simples pasos

Aviation

For beginners

Biblioteca
Aeronáutica
aviación en simples pasos

Conforti, Facundo
    Aviación para principiantes / Facundo Conforti. - 1a ed. - Mar del
Plata : Facundo Jorge Conforti, 2022.
    168 p. ; 21 x 3 cm.

    1. Aviación. I. Tìtulo.
    CDD 387.7404

Fecha de Catalogación: 31/12/2022

1ra Edición.

Facundo Conforti, 2023.

Introduction

This work has been developed to bring the main aeronautical content to aviation enthusiasts, students and future pilots and to anyone passionate about the aeronautical field who wants to learn a little more about this fascinating world of civil aviation.

We will learn the main theoretical concepts of aviation. A summary of each aeronautical area, explained in a simple and pleasant way to read, but at the same time, developing the most relevant content in a professional and highly educational way.

What are the airport runways like? Why does an airplane fly? How do the clouds form? What are the different parts of an airplane? How do the aircraft's instruments work? All these questions and many more, will be answered in this entertaining mandatory aeronautical manual for all those who take their first steps in aviation, or are about to do so.

The Aeronautical Library has more than 60 books published, which makes it the largest Spanish Aeronautical Library in the world!

Capt. Facundo Conforti

Main

Chapter 1 – The airport

Chapter 2 – The aircraft

Chapter 3 – The sky

Chapter 4 – Operations

Chapter 1

The airport

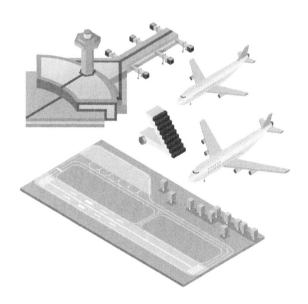

Definition

Airports are defined as a surface of land or water intended for aircraft takeoff and landing operations. They offer different additional functions such as: passenger boarding, cargo boarding, customs services, medical emergencies, firefighting service, airport security services (police), Aero sports institutions, flight schools, and any other function that may arise as necessary in the aeronautical field.

Airports are divided into three categories depending on their main activities, which can be a military aviation airport, an airport for commercial aviation or an airport for general aviation. In some particular cases, there is a mixed airport class where these three classifications coexist together, or just two of them.

For its part, ICAO classifies airports as follows:

• Small airports

• Local airports

• Domestic airports

• International airports

• Transcontinental airports

• Transoceanic airports

• Heliports

In addition to this classification, all airports have other classifications based on various factors. The most common classification is according to operations. Considering this factor, an airport is classified into two parts, a flight section and a ground section. The first refers to the sector where all air operations are carried out, while the second refers to the sector where all passenger operations are carried out.

Each airport can opt for a specific design or diagram according to its needs and the geography of the terrain. There are some standardized models that offer to optimize operations as much as possible. The primary benefit of an adequate airport diagram is to achieve an adequate passenger flow to the traffic presented by the airport, considering this factor as the main factor when deciding on one of the following possible diagrams:

Airport designs

Straight or pier diagram: This diagram surged in the 1950s, giving rise to new methods for mobilizing the flow of passengers. The diagram rose one on one with the airlines when

they implemented individual departure lounges for each flight instead of using common departure lounges. This allows passengers to be served in sectors that are in the same place as the plane during boarding.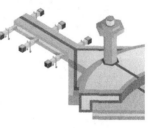

Circular diagram: This diagram offers greater maneuverability of aircraft and greater parking space. A central terminal allows passengers to be connected to the entrances, exits,

counters, customs section and baggage withdrawal. Another benefit of this diagram compared to the previous one is the shorter distances that the passenger flow must travel. Aircraft are concentrated at a single point, which offers the possibility of using shared facilities.

11

Linear diagram: A simple but functional diagram. It is a building in a straight line, where passengers enter on one side and parked aircraft are located on the other side. This diagram, simple and practical, offers direct contact between passengers, boarding and aircraft at all times. Although it is designed for small airports, there are some in particular high traffic airports that use this diagram by joining several terminals in order to maintain the simplicity of the diagram but increasing capacity.

Transported diagram: This diagram is similar to the previous one, except that the boarding lounges are only holding rooms where passengers wait for the transport that will take them to the door of the aircraft. From an operational point of view, this diagram offers many advantages, since aircraft can be parked away from the terminal avoiding towing operations with the cost reduction that this implies.

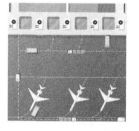

Runway markings

The diagram of runway markings is divided into three large groups. Markings for visual approach runway, markings for non-precision approach runway and markings for precision approach runway.

Each of these groups has a set of specific markings that help the pilot identify the information that the runway offers, both during the final approach and landing and during the takeoff stage. It is essential that every pilot understands the information of the runway markings in order to ensure safety in operations.

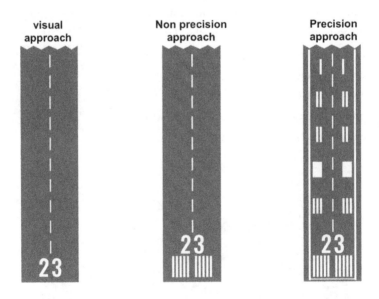

Visual approach runway: This category of runway offers a precarious but sufficient reference for the type of approach for which it is intended. At the beginning of the runway, the numerical designation of the runway with respect to the magnetic north is indicated, and there is an intermittent line that crosses the entire length of the runway in order to offer a visual guide to the center of it. It is a typical runway diagram of uncontrolled airfields, aeroclubs and private runway, where they can be found on lawn surfaces or on paved surfaces. In addition to the primary markings, each aerodrome can add a night beacon system in order to offer this service, even if this does not change the category of the runway.

Non-precision approach runway: A runway diagram that is similar to the previous one but adding additional information at the beginning of it. In this case, a mark of the threshold of the runway identified with parallel bars that inform the width of the runway is included. These bars are divided into two groups, one on each side of the center of the runway and they must have a length of 150 feet (45 meters) in all cases. To obtain the value of the runway width, all the bars included in the two groups are considered and the following measurement information is taken as a reference:

15

RUNWAY WIDTH

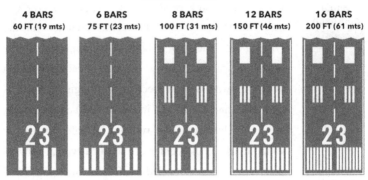

4 BARS	6 BARS	8 BARS	12 BARS	16 BARS
60 FT (19 mts)	75 FT (23 mts)	100 FT (31 mts)	150 FT (46 mts)	200 FT (61 mts)

It is worth mentioning that runways intended for non-precision approaches have a limited runway width, and runways for precision approaches offer the largest number of meters in their width, because operations are carried out by larger and heavier aircraft that require more runway, both longer and wide. This image represents a threshold of 16 bars showing its size with respect to the size of the aircraft.

The following images represent a threshold of 8 bars and a threshold of 12 bars.

Precision approach

Precision approach runway: This runway diagram offers as many markings as possible on a runway. Compared to the previous diagrams, it offers the numerical designation of the runway, the center line that crosses the total length of the runway, the width of it represented by bars, and it adds more visual references such as: the marking of the edges of the runway, the markings of the contact area or "Touchdown Zone" and the "aim" or "Aiming Point". These two concepts are indispensable for the pilot during the final approach.

Zona de touchdown and aiming point: These two visual references are indispensable for a final approach where the pilot needs to know the location of the portion of the runway where he must make contact with the surface and have a fixed point to which to direct his gaze while landing. The "Touchdown Zone TDZ" is a portion of the runway represented with bars parallel to each other. In this section of the runway, the aircraft must make contact with the surface so that the length of the remaining runway is sufficient to carry out the braking action.

The "aim" reference helps the pilot to direct his gaze there with the intention that the aircraft makes contact right at that point, considering a perfect glide path.

17

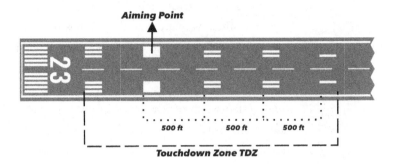

Aiming Point

500 ft   500 ft   500 ft

Touchdown Zone TDZ

As can be seen in this image, the "Aiming Point" is part of the TDZ and only offers a single position on the runway. On the other hand, the TDZ is represented by several groups of parallel bars starting with two groups of three, then two groups of two that are repeated once (in this case) and finally, two individual bars indicating the end of the contact area. The standard distance between each of these groups is approximately 500 feet or 153 m.

Displaced threshold: The threshold of the runway is the edge where it starts and is represented by the numerical designation and the information bars of its width, in case it has this information. For various reasons, the threshold of the runway can be moved forward from its original position and this modification must be informed by markings on the surface of the runway.

There are many reasons why a threshold could be displaced, the most common can be: a deterioration in the surface pavement in this area, which would cause the runway to be moved forward to

18

discard this poor surface, a modification of the glide path by obstacles in the final section which would also cause the displacement of the threshold forward to be able to overcome the obstacles with the same glide path.

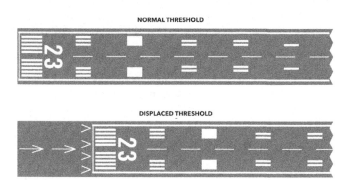

Modifying the location of the runway threshold, the runway length will also be modified, reducing the operational capacity of aircraft that require a minimum number of meters of runway length to operate. The image represents the same runway with the threshold in its original position and the threshold moved forward. This displacement is represented with marks on the displaced surface, indicating with arrows the direction of landing and triangles indicating the new beginning of the runway.

Stopway: Before the start of the runway threshold, there is a paved area of similar characteristics to the surface of the runway that is used as a stop zone or "Stopway" for aircraft landing on the opposite side of the runway in question, that is, a stop zone on runway 23 will be transformed into the "Stopway" of runway 05.

19

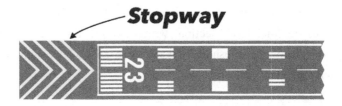

This stop zone is represented by yellow arrows following the direction of the runway landing and is not prepared or available for aircraft operations, either in landing or taxiing operations. This portion of the runway is not taken into account as the available runway length.

Taxiway markings

The marking scheme on the taxiways is based on a central guide line by which the aircraft must direct its nose wheel in order to maintain the center of the paved surface. This guide line is yellow with a black background. It crosses all the taxiways from the parking position of the aircraft to the point of entry to the runway.

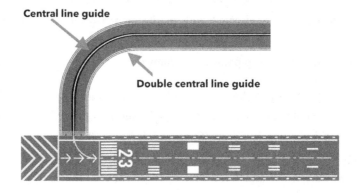

The edges of the taxiway are identified with a double yellow line that does not function as an operation guide, but as information on the operational limit of the paved taxiway.

In addition to the reference of the central guide line, in some sectors of the taxiways, this line is improved with additional broken lines in order to report a particular situation within the taxiway and are called "Enhanced Taxiway Centerline". They can be found at intersections of two or more taxiways, sharp curves, proximity to the entrance to the runway and in any other sector where it is necessary to warn the pilot about the operation during taxiing.

Identification of taxiways: All taxiways are identified with a name composed of a letter, and in some cases, adding a number. This identification is marked on the pavement with the yellow name inside a box with a black background. In case the taxiway crosses another, this one is also indicated on the pavement but with its black identification inside a yellow box and an arrow indicating its direction.

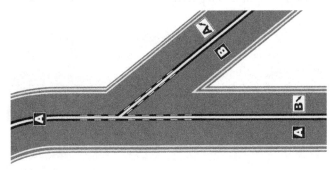

The following image shows an example of the identifying markings of each taxiway. The example on the left indicates that it is the B1 taxiway and reports that at the front are B and H taxiways. The example on the right identifies taxiway Z and indicates that to the right of it is taxiway B, while on the left are taxiways B2 and H.

Identification of runway: When a taxiway is approaching to a runway or intersection of another taxiway and a runway, it is reported with a mark on the pavement indicating the number of runway in white on a red background.

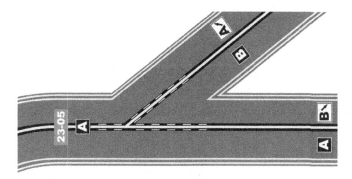

This identification can be found in two ways. On the one hand, it is possible to find a marking on the pavement that indicates the takeoff runway at the front (a single runway number). On the other hand, it is possible to find a double indication of the runway when the taxiway has to cross it through the center of it or another sector other than the beginning of the runway.

23

Another way to announce the proximity to a runway marked on the pavement is to indicate this situation with the RWY AHEAD message.

Identification of a holding point: When a taxiway is approaching to a runway, the pilot encounters a marking on the pavement indicating a mandatory holding point, where he must stop until he obtains the respective traffic control clearance to be able to continue. This point known as "Holding Point" is named before the runway in question. For example, the holding point on runway 23 is called "Holding Point RWY23".

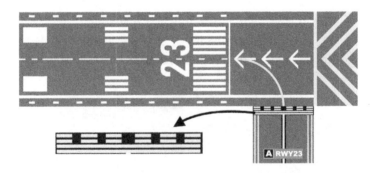

The marking of the holding point has two senses, one of entry to the runway and the other of exit to the runway. When the aircraft approaches the marking of continuous lines, the pilot must

24

have the authorization of traffic control to be able to continue and enter the runway. At this point, the aircraft stops completely until it obtains authorization.

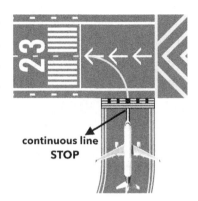

continuous line
STOP

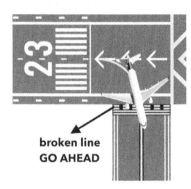

broken line
GO AHEAD

On the other hand, when the aircraft approaches the marking of the holding point from inside the runway, it will encounter the broken lines and will be able to continue to the taxiway without the prior authorization of traffic control.

Lighting system

The lighting system of an airport is one of the bases of operational safety. The body responsible for standardizing this system is ICAO (international civil aviation organization). In order for an airport to be enabled for night operations or operations with reduced visibility, a series of standard lighting systems are established for all areas of the aerodrome, including the area of the visual approach to the runway.

The lighting system of an airport is based on the complexity of its architecture, and based on it a certain lighting system is planned according to the needs of this airport.

The lighting system or "beacon" of an airport is composed of a certain number of "beacons" of different colors for each area, considering the following:

- Runway lights

- Taxiway lights.

- Final approach lights

- Apron lights.

The beacons are located on the surface of the pavement, which can be in the form of a floor lamp, or in the form of a mine under the pavement.

26

As a general rule, the standardized color code includes: green, red, yellow, blue and white and are applied to each of the aforementioned areas.

Runway lights

The runway light system guides the pilot during the takeoff and landing run. This light system offers different types of information, from the remaining distance of the runway, to the indication of the contact area or "touchdown zone".

Each segment of the runway has its own light system based on a certain color code. Each of these segments has its own name and its lighting system is independent of the rest, that is, in the event of the failure of one of them, the rest will continue to work normally.

The runway light system has three levels of intensity, low, medium and high. The intensity is operated from the control tower and can be modified at the pilot's request, depending on the weather conditions at the time of operation.

Runway edge lights

The runway edge lights include the lights on the sides of the runway and the lights on the center line of the runway. This light system has three levels of intensity. Low intensity or LIRL (light intensity runway light). Medium intensity or MIRL (medium intensity runway light). High intensity or HIRL (high intensity runway light). This system of lights is white, except for the side lights in the last 600 meters where they are represented as yellow.

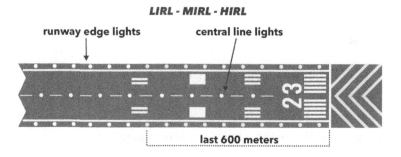

LIRL - MIRL - HIRL

runway edge lights   central line lights

last 600 meters

Touchdown zone lights

The contact zone lights or the touchdown zone are known as TDZL (touchdown zone lights) and are set for runway enabled for ILS operations categories II and III. This light system starts at the runway threshold and extends to the first 900 meters of length of the runway. They are beacons in the form of mines located under the pavement and they illuminate the area in white.

Touchdown Zone Light TDZL

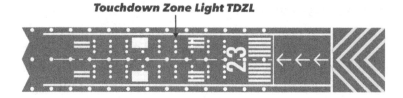

Center line lights for ILS

The center line lights of the runway for ILS operations offer a guide for all ILS operations categories II and III, or for take-off procedures where the RVR value is less than 400 meters. These runway center line (RCL) go from threshold to threshold, mainly considering the white color, except in the last 900 meters where white and red lights interact indicating that the end of the runway is approaching. The last 300 meters will be identified only with red lights in order to alert pilots to the remaining runway.

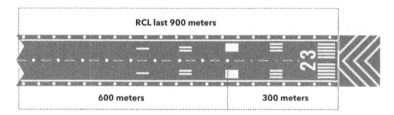

Runway ending identifier lights

The lights at the end of the runway are composed of a device similar to the previous one, in the form of a mine and bidirectional lights. In the case of runway ending identifier light, the beacon emits a red light in the direction of the final approach alerting the pilot to the location of the end of the runway. This light system is known as REIL (runway end identifier lights). On the other side of the

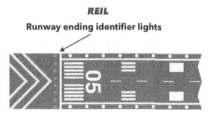

29

beacon, a green light is emitted indicating the beginning of the runway threshold.

Runway threshold lights

The runway threshold lights work in conjunction with the REIL lights, in most cases they work with the same special two-light beacon, but indicating a green light signal to inform the start of the runway. When there is a displacement of the runway threshold, these lights must be located at the beginning of the displaced threshold. They point unidirectionally toward the final approach and their intensity can be graduated from the control tower.

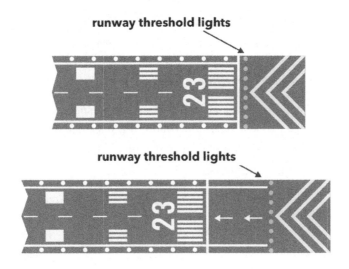

30

Stopway lights

The lights on the stopway or stop zone are red and single-way, illuminating toward the aircraft's takeoff run in order to warn pilots of this area during this journey, or about the landing run indicating the remaining area for emergency braking. This light system includes lights at the edge of the area and at the end of it.

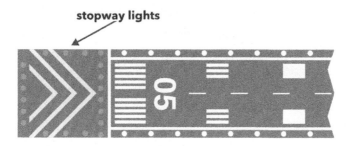

Taxiway edge lights

The lighting system at the edge of the taxiways is composed of traditional blue beacons that surround the taxiways, platforms and ground operation areas of the aircraft.

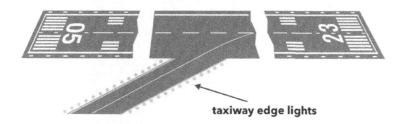

Taxiway center line lights

The central light system of the taxiways is mine-type and green. Located on the yellow central guide line on the taxiway, they carry the aircraft along the airport to the apron or to the runway.

taxiway center line lights

Holding point lights

The holding point light system is known as STOP BARS. It is a set of mine-type beacons that are illuminated red prohibiting the passage of aircraft. This system is usually at the holding points before entering the runway in order to maintain an orderly operation on it. Stop bars will be required for all operations when the value of the RVR is less than 350 meters.

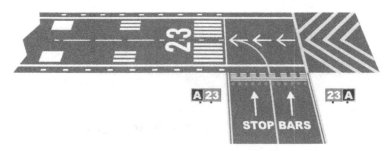

Approach Lighting System (ALS)

An instrumental approach to a runway consists of two instances, one based on the radio approach instruments and the other on systems for a guided visual approach to the runway. This is because most instrumental approaches reaches a certain point where the pilot must continue with a visual approach until landing, except in ILS category III approaches, where a visual final stage is not required and the aircraft can make an automatic landing without visibility, known as "Autoland".

The sudden change from the instrumental approach phase to the visual approach phase is a challenge that the pilot must overcome while maintaining the flight parameters that he had been controlling until now. For this, there are runway lighting systems that help the pilot to follow a light signal until he makes visual contact with the surface of the runway.

There are several approach light systems. Each aerodrome will determine which of all these systems is correct for the approach to its runway. In some cases, there are specific approach light systems for ILS Cat II-III operations, and even approach light systems for situations where a final approach in turn is necessary.

ALS systems are divided into two groups, the systems that guide the pilot on the horizontal path and the systems that guide the pilot on the vertical path.

ALSF system (Approach Lighting System Sequenced Flashing Lights): This system is characterized by having a series of flashing lights that guide the pilot on his correct route on the extension of the central axis of the runway until he reaches it. There are two kinds of this system and their difference is in the number of visual references that each one has. It is worth mentioning that the more equipped the approach light system is, the easier it will be to guide the pilot in the case of conditions of extremely low visibility.

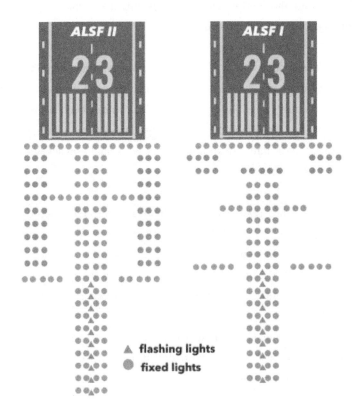

34

MALS system (medium approach lighting system): It is a lighting system of medium intensity and less complexity than the previous one, typical of smaller aerodromes where the meteorological factor is not so restrictive for approaches and landings. This system offers two variants, one with an alignment indicator to the center of the runway and the other with this indicator and a flashing light sequence system.

MALSR system (MALS with Rwy Alignment indicator): This variant of the system offers a visual indication of the route to the center of the runway along with an alignment indicator on the central axis of the runway. In this case, the alignment system of the central axis of the runway is not integrated into the main system but is prior to it in order to reach the final visual guide with the aircraft centered on the main axis of the runway.

MALSF system (MALS with sequenced flashing lights): This variant of the system is identical to the previous one but adds a system of flashing lights that guide the pilot on the correct route on the central axis of the runway. In this case, the flashing system is incorporated into the main light system.

35

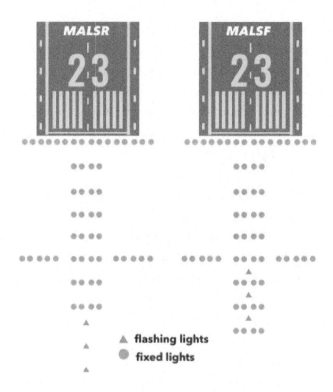

▲ flashing lights
● fixed lights

PAPI (Precision Approach Path Indicator): This system is one of the most used in most airports in the world. It offers a precise descent slope to the surface of the runway or contact area. This glide path is usually graduated on a slope of 3° or 3.5° depending on the slope that seeks to be established at that airport. Its range capacity is around 20 NM depending on the intensity of light emitted by the equipment. Its operating principle is very simple, it consists of four headlights aligned side by side of the runway. These headlights emit three-colored lights: white, green and red.

The combination of these colored lights will tell the pilot if he is on the correct glide path, above it or below it.

Above the glide path: When the aircraft is flying completely above the correct glide path, the PAPI system indicates all its white lights.

Slightly above the glide path: When the aircraft is flying slightly above the correct glide path, the PAPI system indicates three white lights and one red light.

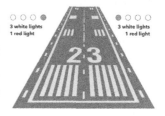

On the right glide path: When the aircraft is flying over the correct glide path, the PAPI system indicates two white lights and two red lights.

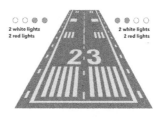

Slightly below the glide path: When the aircraft is flying slightly below the correct glide path, the PAPI system indicates three red lights and one white light.

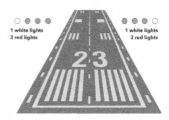

37

Below the glide path: When the aircraft is flying completely below the correct glide path, the PAPI system indicates four red lights.

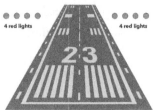

Signal system

The signal system inside an airport is a pillar of operational safety. From ground personnel known as "marshall" to the most sophisticated digital signage systems are part of a set of tools available to guide pilots in different situations, from a taxi, a start-up or an emergency situation in flight.

The following are the three main sources of standard signage within an airport:

- Ground signaling (signs or ground personnel)

- Digital signage on the ground

- In-flight signaling (tower - airplane - tower signals)

Signaling on ground

Signal functions by ground personnel have evolved over the years. In the beginning, airline personnel guided the aircraft on the ground with their hands making signals in order to position the aircraft at a certain point to which pilots did not have visual access

38

from the cockpit. The constant advance in the aeronautics industry led to the improvement of these techniques by implementing tools such as flashlights and signal bars in order to be able to offer the service under conditions of reduced visibility.

The main function of the ground personnel in charge of the signals is to guide the aircraft on the correct route to the desired position by means of standardized signals. In some large airports where traffic congestion requires it, it is possible to find the figure of "wingwalker" or wing-head signaler. These are additional ground personnel who check the movement of the aircraft and avoid collision with others.

Wingwalker Position: In this position, the signaler warns the rest of the ground personnel and the pilot about the free movement of the aircraft. The procedure consists of keeping the right arm elevated with the signaling tool and with the left arm generating an upward and downward lateral movement without exceeding the height of the shoulder or exceeding the position of the left leg.

Position Identification: Located right in front of the assigned parking position, the signaler informs the pilot that it is the correct position in order to avoid confusion with the rest of the positions. The procedure is based on moving his arms straight from top to bottom with his hands and signaling tools straight, always facing the aircraft so that the pilot understands that he must approach the signaler.

Indication of movement: With this signage, ground personnel communicate that the aircraft must go to another signaler in the direction indicated by its movement. In case there is no signal in the vicinity, this movement indicates that you follow the instructions of the control. The procedure is performed with both arms from above, going down to one side to shoulder height.

Continue ahead: Once the aircraft is already facing the right position, the signaler tells you to continue braking until it tells you to stop. This procedure is performed with his arms outstretched and shaking the forearm from the center up again and again. It is worth mentioning that this indication not only implies that the aircraft must remain at the front, but must also do so on the central yellow line. In case of any deviation, the signaler will warn the pilot.

Deviation corrections: In the event that the aircraft departs from the central yellow line of the taxiway, the signaler will tell the pilot the direction in which the nose train must turn in order to return to the correct position. This procedure is performed in two ways, depending on the side to be corrected.

If the aircraft has to turn left (view from the cockpit), the signaler will keep his right arm straight and parallel to the ground, while with his left arm he will make a 90° movement from top to bottom to shoulder height.

If the aircraft must turn right (view from the cockpit), the signaler will keep his left arm straight and parallel to the ground, while with his right arm he will make a 90° movement from top to bottom to shoulder height.

Faced with the possibility of a new deviation, the signaler will be able to alternate the movements until it manages to take the aircraft to the center of the central yellow line.

Normal stop: Once the aircraft is reaching the end point of the movement, the signaler slowly informs you that the time to stop is approaching in order to avoid sudden braking of the aircraft. The

procedure begins with both arms extended and parallel to the ground and as the aircraft approaches the end point, the arms are raised until they are crossed over the head of the signaler indicating to the pilot that he must already stop walking.

Abnormal stop: In case of any situation that puts the safety of the operation at risk, the signaler can inform the pilot that he must stop immediately. The procedure is based on performing a 90° movement crossing the arms above the head over and over again as a sign of an abnormal situation.

Brakes indication: When arriving at the final position and stopping the plane, the pilot must activate the brakes at the time the signaler informs him that he will no longer need any other movement of the aircraft. This procedure consists of keeping one arm extended and parallel to the body while raising the hand of the other arm to shoulder height with the palm open and when indicating the activation of the brakes, the palm is closed leaving the cuff closed until the pilot confirms the activated brake.

45

In the opposite situation, where the aircraft is about to start its movement, the pilot must release the brakes when the signaler informs him that there are no obstacles to start the movement. This procedure is similar to the previous one but begins with a closed fist and ends with an open palm.

Wheel chocks: The movement of wheel chocks has two purposes, on the one hand, to prevent unwanted movement of the aircraft and on the other hand, to allow the aircraft to start its movement without obstacles. In the first case, the ground staff places the wheel chocks between the wheels of the landing gear to prevent their displacement. In the second case, the ground personnel remove the wheel chocks and free up the space between the wheels of the train and the surface of the pavement.

The movement of placed wheel chocks is carried out with the two arms extended and the signaling tools pointing inward, from this position, the signaler carries the arms from the outside to the inside until the markers are joined.

The movement of released wheel chocks is similar to the previous one but with the pointers pointing outwards and a movement from the inside out, inverse to the previous one.

Engine operation: To maximize operational safety, ground personnel must notify the pilot when the ignition area of the engines is free. This procedure is performed by lifting the right arm to head height and making circles, while the left arm raised diagonally indicates with your hand the number of engines to start.

On the other hand, when the aircraft has reached its final position and stopped, it's time to turn off the engines. Ground personnel must confirm that the shutdown of the engines has been successful so that all the rest of the personnel can approach the aircraft. This

48

procedure is based on lifting one arm and indicating with your hand the number of motors to be checked and with the other arm making a movement from one shoulder to the other at the height of the neck with the signaling tool, as if you were drawing a straight line between one shoulder and the other.

Reduce speed: Normally, the taxi speed at the time of entering the parking position should be the same as that of a person walking. When ground personnel consider that the aircraft is overshooting speed at the time of entering the position, they must instruct the pilot to slow down in order to maximize the safety of the operation.

It may indicate that it slows down on both engines by making an upward and downward movement with both arms at the same time. Or, it can indicate that the pilot reduces the speed of one engine, leaving the engine arm with the correct speed glued to the body, and moving the arm of the engine side from top to bottom that must reduce the speed.

49

Fire indications: Fire is one of the most dangerous factors when operating an aircraft on the ground. Ground personnel must immediately notify the pilot in case they see fire or smoke in any of the engines or braking systems, these two being the most common places where fire can occur due to the high temperatures they usually handle. This procedure is based on making circles with the right arm drawing an eight over the air while the left arm indicates the area where the fire is, the left arm above indicates fire in the engine and the left arm below indicates fire in the brake system.

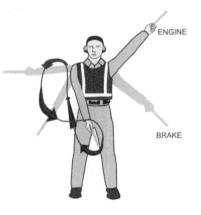

50

Hold position: Sometimes ground personnel need the aircraft to maintain the position for a few moments until all the signaling tasks are completed. To indicate this request, ground personnel will keep their arms outstretched diagonally and downwards.

GPU operation (ground power unit): To save fuel and be able to shut down the aircraft's turbines, airlines usually provide their aircraft with ground equipment that offers electrical and pneumatic power to supply the aircraft externally while its engines and APU are turned off. The operation of this auxiliary unit is coordinated between the pilot and ground personnel, both for the connection and for the disconnection of the equipment with the aircraft.

The signaling procedure for the connection is based on extending the palm of one hand horizontally and the palm of the other hand vertically just below the previous one and making an upward movement simulating the connection of the hands.

51

In the opposite case, the signaling procedure for disconnection will be the other way around. One palm extended horizontally and the other vertically attached to the previous one but making a downward movement simulating a disconnection.

Establish communication: Communication between ground personnel and the cockpit is carried out through an intercom system of each aircraft. For this procedure, both the pilot and the ground staff request the connection of the system by bringing their hands to their heads and covering their ears.

Stairs operation: Some aircraft models have their own stairs for the descent of passengers. Ground personnel must inform the pilot that the area of operation of the ladder is free of obstacles and can now be extended. For this procedure, he raises his left arm 45° above his head and with his right arm he makes a diagonal movement from his left shoulder to the lower right sector. Other common signals are those made by the pilot towards ground personnel. For the same purpose as the previous ones, try to warn the signaler of a particular situation or requirement.

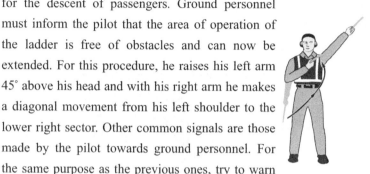

Activated brakes: The pilot raises his arm to shoulder height with his fingers outstretched and makes a movement to close his fist indicating that the brakes have been connected.

Disable brakes: Similar to the previous one, with the arm at shoulder height, it starts with the cuff closed and performs a movement to extend your fingers and completely open the palm indicating that the brakes have been released.

Placement of wheel chocks: In order to request the placement of the shoes, the pilot raises his arms vertically and with his palms outstretched making a movement from the outside to the inside.

Release chocks: To request the release of the shoes, the pilot performs a movement similar to the previous one but from the inside out.

Engine start: When the pilot has performed all the pre-start-up procedures, he must notify ground personnel of his intention to start a certain engine. To do this, he raises his hand and indicates with his fingers, the number of motors to be turned on.

Digital signage on the ground

With the advancement of technology, the aeronautical industry has been improving its tools year after year. From analog flight decks to digital flight decks and from manual signaling on the ground by trained personnel to a digital system capable of fulfilling the same functions with extreme precision.

Looking for a constant optimization of resources, a digital signage system known as VDGS (visual docking guidance system) was created. This system offers different variables that adapt to the needs of each airport:

AGNIS system (azimuth guidance nose in stands): This system offers an alignment of the nose of the aircraft that enters the parking position on the yellow center line. Work together with other tools such as side indications and a Mirror System at the front so that the pilot can see the right point where he must stop walking.

Its operating principle is based on a box with two vertical bars of green and red lights. When the aircraft is set on the yellow center line, the system will indicate two green bars if the aircraft's nose is correctly aligned to enter the position. In case of any deviation from this alignment, the system will indicate a red and a green light bar. The three possible indications are described below:

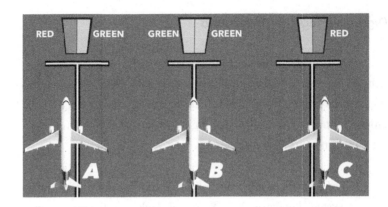

In this image, three aircraft are entering to the parking position. Aircraft B has its nose correctly aligned to the central yellow line and the system indicates two green lights. On the other hand, aircraft A is moved to the left of the center line and the system indicates a left red light and a right green light indicating the deviation and where it should make the correction. Aircraft C has the same situation as aircraft A but with a detour to the other side.

APIS system (aircraft positioning information system): This system offers more complete and detailed information than the previous one. A set of yellow alphanumeric characters with a black background inform about the number of the position, the model of the aircraft authorized upon entry, any lateral deviation from the center running line and the progress of the approach of the aircraft from 16 meters away from the final position to the exact position where it should stop. This digital signage system is divided into two. The upper section represented with alphanumeric characters and the lower section represented with a bar and point diagram. The operation of each section is detailed below.

Upper section: The upper section can report in alphanumeric characters the type of aircraft, the position number, the flight number, the remaining distance to the final position and the textual indication of Stop.

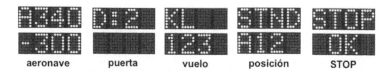

| aeronave | puerta | vuelo | posición | STOP |

Lower section: : The lower section is divided into two types of information. On the one hand, the indication of deviations by means of bars and arrows; and on the other hand, the indication of zooming through a dotted rectangle as seen in the examples below:

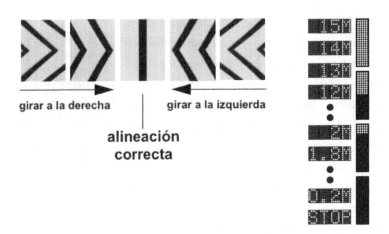

girar a la derecha | girar a la izquierda

alineación correcta

Safedock system: This system is similar to the previous one but offers all the information in the same section. Aircraft model, position number, lateral deviation and approach from the taxiway to the stop line. The following image details the sequence of information offered by this system until it reaches the final position.

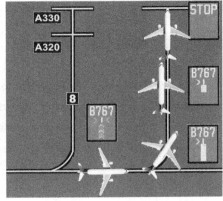

Chapter 2

The aircraft

Introduction

The structure of the aircraft comprises the main structural elements of the aircraft that support the loads to which the aircraft is subjected in the air and on the ground. The main components are the fuselage, the wings, the tail assembly and the flight controls.

The fuselage

The fuselage is the main structure or body of the aircraft. Take passengers and crews in safe and comfortable conditions. The fuselage also provides space for controls, accessories and other equipment. It transfers loads to and from the main planes or wings, the aircraft, the fins, the landing gear and, in certain configurations, the engines. There are three main types of fuselage construction. First there is the type of armor or frame that is usually used for light and non-pressurized aircraft.

Then there is the monocoque construction, which was mainly used at the beginning of the 20th century. Finally, there is the semi-monosque fuselage that is used in most non-pressurized aircraft.

Armor fuselage or frame: When a frame structure is used for the fuselage, the frame consists of light steel tubes of minimum wall thickness that are joined to form a triangular-shaped spatial frame. This gives the most rigid geometric shapes. Each tube carries a specific load, the magnitude of which depends on whether the aircraft is in the air or on the ground. This type of manufacturing is strong, easy to build and provides a relatively problem-free basic arrangement.

The frame is usually covered by a lightweight aluminum alloy or a fabric skin to form a closed and aerodynamically efficient cargo transport compartment. The most characteristic example of this type of fuselage is the classic PIPER aircraft, the PA-11 model.

Monocoque fuselage: Monocoque is a French word that means "unique helmet". In a monococcal structure all charges are absorbed by a stressed skin with only light frames or internal trainers to give the required shape. Due to its structure characteristics, even slight damage to the surface can seriously weaken the structure. To be a true monocoque, the structure would not have openings at all, like an ostrich egg; but for practical purposes, in an airplane, openings must be provided for access and maintenance.

The openings must be reinforced to maintain the integrity of the structure. But, once the aircraft doors are closed and all the hatches and access panels are installed, the fuselage is, for all intents and purposes, a monocoque structure. Two planes built according to the monocoque principle were the Roland CII plywood construction (1915) and the Ford Trimotor (1926).

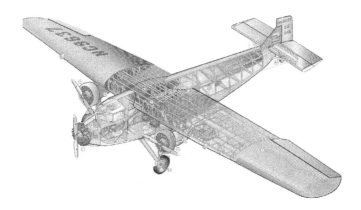

Semi-single-hull fuselage: As the planes grew larger and the air loads increased, it was found that the pure monocoque structure was not strong enough. Additional structural limbs known as lves were added to run along the length along the fuselage joining the frames. Then a light alloy leather was joined to the frames and strips by riveting or adhesive bonding. This type of fuselage construction was called semi-monocoque.

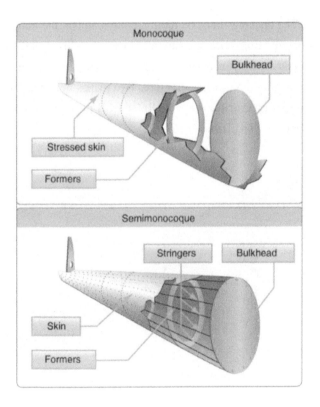

In the semi-single-hull fuselages, the stringers and frames harden the skin (surface or wall), and the flight loads are shared between the skin and the structure underneath. The bulkheads are placed in place to separate the different sections of the fuselage; for example, between the engine compartment and the passenger compartment.

The bulkhead has the same basic shape as the frames or trainers, but it almost completely isolates one compartment from the other. However, you have to make holes in the bulkhead. These allow the control accessories, pipes and electrical cables to pass through the length of the fuselage. The bulkheads are usually built much more substantially than the frames because they are subject to greater loads. In addition, the bulkhead that separates the engine from the passenger compartment and serves to delay the passage of the engine fire backwards, in case a fire breaks.

The choice of the type of fuselage responds to the purpose of the aircraft and is decided by the manufacturer. The fuselage is considered the skeleton of the aircraft, and must be selected correctly according to the type of flight assigned to each aircraft.

Wings

Let's start with the most important aerodynamic structure of the plane, the wings. Most of the aerodynamic forces acting in flight overturn on them and are the causes of the aerodynamic effect that enable the plane to move through the air. As we have mentioned in previous pages, the wings are composed of a sequence of aerodynamic profiles side by side, along the entire wing surface.

The number of profiles will define the total surface of the wings and their length, which is known as "Wingspan" (distance between the two ends of the wings). Considering that the larger the wingspan, the greater the wing surface, and as a result, the greater the lift, unlike a smaller wingspan.

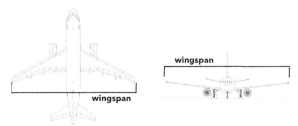

The manufacturer of each aircraft defines the wingspan of his aircraft according to the purpose of the aircraft, as well as decides what type of wings he will manufacture for the model. We can classify the wings according to the following variables:

- The position with respect to the fuselage of the aircraft.
- The number of Wings or planes on the same plane.
- The angle of the "arrow" or wing shape.
- The angle or "dihedral" of the wings.
- The specific shape of each wing.

67

The first classification is based on the position of the wings with respect to the fuselage and can be:

High Wing   /   Middle Wing   /   Low Wing

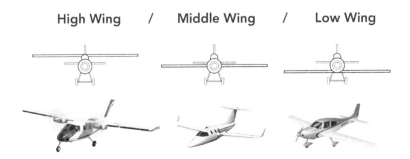

Each of these classifications refers to the position of the wings with respect to the fuselage of the aircraft. In addition, the wings can have more than one plane on their structure.

Monoplane   /   Biplane   /   Triplane   /   Multiplane

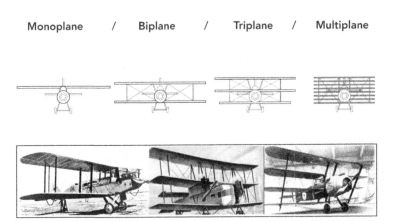

Another classification is based on the "arrow" position of the design of each wing, this being the angle formed by the wing and the transverse axis of the aircraft.

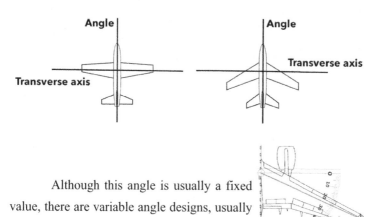

Although this angle is usually a fixed value, there are variable angle designs, usually assigned to fighter jets.

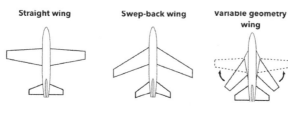

Another common variable in the manufacture of wings is the "dihedral" or the angle formed by the surface of the plane (wing) and the line of the royal horizon.

69

Finally, the specific shape of the wing is also defined by the manufacturer. Depending on the purpose of the flights planned by the aircraft, the manufacturer can opt for one of the following wing models:

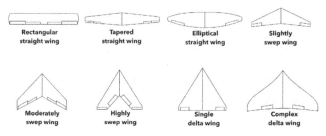

Ailerons and Elevator

The aileron system is made up of two aluminum surfaces located at the end of each wing. The ailerons have an asymmetric movement among each other; that is, when the left aileron rises, the right aileron goes down and vice versa. They are operated from the cockpit by means of the control levers, which are mechanically attached to each aileron by pulleys and cables.

70

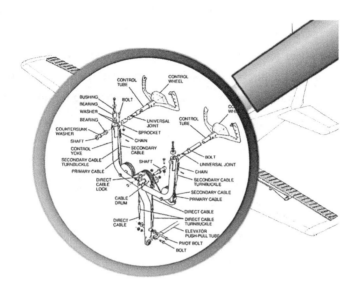

Looking more closely at the entire flight control system, there are two control commands located in the cockpit that are mechanically connected to a system of pulleys and cables that allow the movement not only of the ailerons, but also of the elevator.

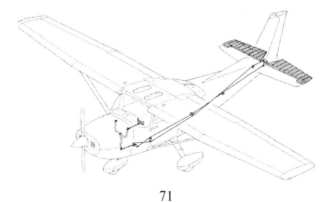

Like the ailerons, the elevator is attached to the controls by means of cables and pulleys, but unlike t h e ailerons, this control system moves to the same side and at the same time, up or down, giving the aircraft the pitching movement. It has a cable and a pulley system for upward movements and another one for downward movements.

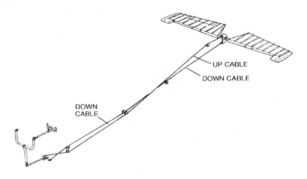

Associated with the elevator system, there is a compensation system known as TRIM installed. It is a wiring device that is attached to a flat surface located in the elevator that helps compensate up or down for the movement of this flight control. It is operated from the cockpit by means of a wheel located under the main panel.

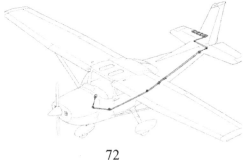

72

Rudder or Steering Rudder

The rudder system has a working principle similar to the previous systems. It is operated from the cockpit by means of a pedal system mechanically linked with cables and pulleys to the control surface located on the empennage on the vertical stabilizer.

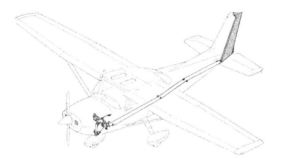

Looking closely, two sets of pedals are located: one set for each pilot. When the pilot exerts force with his foot on one of the pedals, the mechanism of cables and pulleys will move the surface of the rudder to give the plane the yaw movement.

73

Flaps and Slats

FLAPS and SLATS are considered secondary flight controls. Located along the leading edge and the leaking edge, they are considered hight lift devices, that is, these devices can maximize the lift that a wing surface can produce in a certain flight situation.

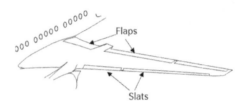

While these two devices fulfill the same function (increasing lift), they do so differently. In the first instance we must understand that the lift can be modified by angle of attack (AOA), wing curvature, wing surface and finally, speed.

On the one hand, SLATS works by modifying the angle of attack (AOA), thus modifying the lift. On the other hand, FLAPS works by modifying the curvature and wing surface, obtaining a modification in the value of the lift.

Let's start by analyzing the structure of SLATS. When this system is activated, the SLAT detaches from the leading edge by means of a mechanical actuator. This enables the wing airfoil to

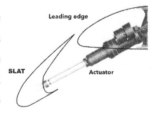

increase its angle of attack without producing a detachment of the airflow delaying the stall speed.

Airflow
AOA without Slats

Airflow
AOA with Slats

There are three types of slats, they can be fixed, automatic or manually operated.

Fixed slats: These devices remain in a fixed and extended position of the leading edge of the profile. On the one hand, they are useful since they do not depend on the pilot's actions. On the other hand, when they are always extended, during the cruise flight stage they present additional resistance to advance.

Automatic slats: These devices are configured to extend automatically at certain stages of flight where the plane is close to reaching a high angle of attack that approaches the stall speed.

Manual slats: This type of device allows the manual operation of the system from inside the cockpit, leaving its operation to the pilot's discretion.

Having understood the slats system, let's now study the operation of one of the most popular and used systems in most aircraft, whatever its size, the flaps system.

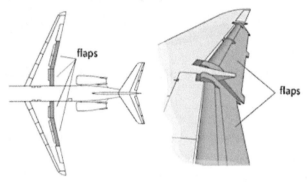

The flaps system can be located on the leading edge or at the trailing edge of the aircraft and are made up of aerodynamic surfaces or fins that extend from the respective edges in order to increase lift due to two variables:

✓ By increasing the curvature of the wing airfoil, generating greater suction (lift) in the upper surface.

✓ By increasing the wing surface, modifying the variable "S" (surface) in the lifting formula and increasing its value.

The size of the FLAPS fins is measured by their curvature and represents 30% of the length of the wing curvature at most, that is, with FLAPS extended, the curvature of the wing increases its surface by an additional 30%. Depending on the purpose of the aircraft, the manufacturer may decide to install different models or types of FLAPS. Let's see the most used:

76

Spoilers

They are considered as a lifting reduction system. This system is composed of aerodynamic surfaces mounted on the extrados on the wing surface and just in front of the Flaps. Its normal position is folded over the contour of the wing. By means of hydraulic activators, their drive leaves them in an almost vertical position and facing directly the relative wind.

SPOILERS

Flaps

When spoilers are driven, they reduce lift and increase resistance in the location area of the device. Whether large or high performance aircraft, spoilers can fulfill three functions:

Balance: In this function the spoilers work together with the spoilers. When the aircraft's automatic system detects a certain inclination angle during a turn, it gradually activates the extension of the spoilers of the wing corresponding to the turn side. This action gives off the limit layer on the extrados of said wing, reduces lift and helps maximize the effect of the spoilers achieving a greater turn with less force load.

Air Brakes: When the spoiler system is manually operated, they extend over the wing between 30° and 35°

77

perpendicular to it generating enormous resistance to advance, and with it, an immediate deceleration of the aircraft. This function is usually used in flight when you want to slow down quickly or when the aircraft requires a steeper descent without increasing its speed. Brakes are a manual function intentionally operated by pilots.

Landing: Unlike the previous function, in this case the spoilers extend over the wing between 50° and 60° perpendicular to it. The objective of this function is to reduce the landing stroke by breaking the boundary layer over the extrados and increasing the advance resistance of the aircraft. Additionally, the capacity of the braking system is greater since there is less lifting on the extrados due to the opening of its limit layer, the wheels of the plane tend to remain firmer on the runway.

Flight instruments

Flight instruments are devices that, through the "interpretation" of different signals, show the crew the values and data necessary to execute the flight, whether instrumental or visual.

The principle of static port and pitot tube

Before developing the operation of the aircraft's instruments, it is necessary to know the fundamental physical basis of the origin of the signals and the measurement methods. To do this, the principle of pitot tubes and static intakes is elaborated below.

Development must begin with a foundation of the fundamental principle, pressure. Pressure is a comparison between two forces. Absolute pressure exists when comparing a force with a total vacuum, or no absolute pressure. It is necessary to define absolute pressure, because the air in the atmosphere always exerts pressure, above all. Even when it seems that no pressure is being applied, such as when a balloon deflates, there is still atmospheric pressure inside and outside the balloon. To measure that atmospheric pressure, it is necessary to compare it with a total absence of pressure, such as that produced in a vacuum. Many aircraft instruments make use of absolute pressure values, such as the altimeter, the ascent speed indicator and the multiple pressure gauge.

The most common type of pressure measurement is the gauge pressure. This expresses the difference between the pressure to be measured and atmospheric pressure. The gauge pressure inside the deflated balloon mentioned above is, therefore, 0 pounds per square inch (psi). The pressure of the pressure gauge is easily measured and obtained by ignoring the fact that the atmosphere always exerts its pressure, above all.

The pitot tube is a device that is used to establish the flow rate through the measurement of stagnation pressure or total pressure. The pressure is measured in a direction parallel to that of the flow and occluded at its other end that is equal to the sum of the static pressure and the dynamic pressure. Static pressure is the pressure of a fluid measured at one point. The total pressure is measured at the clogged end. Therefore, the value of the dynamic pressure that depends on the flow rate and its density is calculated by the difference between the measurements, in this case with the displacement of the diaphragm.

This device is used for flow measurement and consists of two tubes that detect pressure at two different points of the pipe. They can be mounted separately or grouped within a housing, forming a single device. One of the tubes measures the impact pressure at one point in the vein, the other measures only the static pressure, usually through a hole in the conduction wall. A pitot tube measures two pressures simultaneously, impact pressure (pt) and static pressure (ps).

The Bernoulli Principle is the one that allows to establishing the pressure ratio and with it, be able to obtain a fundamental value for flight: aerodynamic speed. Based on the above theory, it can be concluded that the three basic flight instruments are the speedometer, the variometer and the altimeter. The graph below shows its installation in the flight deck of a light aircraft typically used for instruction and training.

Altimeter

An analog altimeter, like the one shown in the previous figure works with the same principle as a clock, with two hands, it works with the same principle as a clock, with two hands. It has a dial marked with numbers from 0 to 9, arranged clockwise, with intermediate divisions. The instrument is made up of a closed cylindrical box, inside which is arranged an aneroid capsule, made of very thin metal (usually copper).

The aneroid capsule is pre-filled with a standard atmospheric pressure (1013.2 Hp or mmHg). The altimeter has a port through which atmospheric pressure enters (from the static intake), therefore,

81

there will be a difference in pressures between the reading of the static intake and that present in the aneroid capsule.

The altimeters have two needles. The longest needle indicates thousands of feet, while the second one indicates hundreds. In this type of altimeter, a full turn of the larger needle indicates that 10,000 feet were won or lost (depending on the direction of rotation). In altimeters that have three needles, the third and shorter indicates tens of a thousand.

According to the previous paragraphs, the altitude reading is a difference in pressures. Therefore, it is necessary that the altimeter be calibrated according to the place of operation of the aircraft and

other operational peculiarities that will be described. To this end, all altimeters have a manual control device that allows the internal aneroid capsule to be dilated or contracted, with the aim of decreasing or increasing the value of the internal reference pressure.

The variation in the volume of the capsule responds to the fundamental principle of Boyle-Marriot that expresses "... the value of the pressure is inversely proportional to the volume...". This calibration is known as an "altimeter setting". To verify the correction value, all altimeters have a graduated window, which allows you to see the adjustment reference; this device is known as the adjustment window or "Kollsman".

The image below shows the cutting of a mechanical analog pressure altimeter; an instrument that equips the vast majority of general aviation aircraft. In the cut, you can see the detail of the aneroid capsule and the mechanical connection with the set of gears and connecting rods that allow the movement and indication to be transmitted to the needles on the quadrant of the instrument.

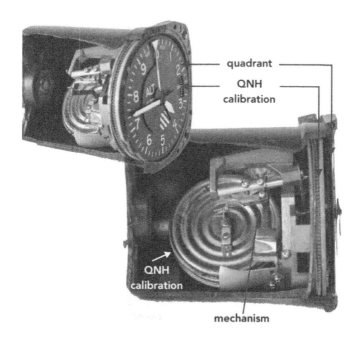

As can be seen in the previous image, the aneroid capsule is located in a closed container (cut of the shell seen in the image) where it receives external pressure, through a flexible duct with connection to the static intake. The actual pressure from the outside will be responsible for the expansion or contraction of the capsule.

The set of gears and associated connecting rods are those that transmit the movement and transform it into a calibrated angular movement; which, in turn, is then transformed into altitude reading for the crew.

For the calibration of the altimeter, it is necessary to consider different pressure values. The values correspond to the place of operation, reference at the level of the evil, and specific pressure of a point. These pressure reference values are expressed as follows:

QNH: it is the value of the pressure referred to sea level. In this case, with the aircraft on the ground, the altimeter will indicate the altitude at which the aerodrome is located.

QNE: it is the representation of the pressure referred to the flight level, that is, it is the adjustment that indicates the distance from the ground to the reference pressure of the aneroid capsule.

QFE: it is the specific pressure at a point in the earth's crust, in the case of the aircraft, it will be the actual pressure that exists at the aerodrome at the time of the start of the operation.

Airspeed indicator

The speedometer or aerodynamic speed indicator is the device that quantifies the relative speed of the aircraft with respect to the air mass where it moves. Aerodynamic speed is an expression of

84

relationships, not a speed of displacement with respect to a point on the ground (ground speed).

The speedometer is a device that measures the pressure differences and transforms them into units of speed (knots, miles per hour, etc.). The differential value between the impact pressure or total pressure and the static pressure value is the value that will be converted into aerodynamic speed. As a general concept for understanding operation, it is said that the greater the pressure difference, the greater the aerodynamic speed.

Like the altimeter, the speedometer has a barometric capsule inside it that maintains the impact pressure inside through a connection port with the pitot tube. The pressure difference between the inside and outside of the aneroid capsule generates shrinkage or expansion of the material. This movement is captured by the internal clockwork system that translates it into the movement of the hand on the dial of the instrument.

Just as the example of the altimeter was made, below is an image of a fully disassembled speedometer in its sealed container housing. In this case, it is observed that the pressure census capsule is located on the back of the instrument. At the back of the capsule there are two ports through which the pressure of the impact air mass and the static pressure enter.

85

Through that pressure, the instrument generates the expansion and contraction of the capsule, which transmits the movement towards the gears and set of internal connecting rods; which will then be responsible for generating the angular movement of the only needle that will move in the graduated quadrant (in this case the reading is done in miles per hour, along with a dial that allows you to see the conversion into knots).

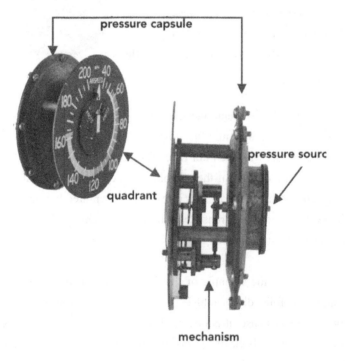

aguja sobre el cuadrante

Variometer

It is the flight instrument that provides information related to two variables of the aircraft, closely related to each other: the movement of ascent or descent and the regime or rate with which it does so, better known as vertical speed.

The operating principle of the variometer is similar to that of the altimeter. The marking on the dial is generated by the contraction and expansion movement of an aneroid capsule in contact with the external pressure of the air. The difference with the altimeter is that the variometer does not measure the absolute pressure, but records the pressure changes coming from the static intake of the fuselage; it does not need dynamic pressure reading. The set of aneroid capsule and watch system is located inside a closed and insulated container, in the same way as the speedometer and the altimeter.

The variometer has a single needle that marks on a dial with a scale that begins at zero (located to the left of the quadrant of the instrument). The reading is simple, all the marks that are above zero indicate ascent, while those located below show a descent regime. In light aircraft, varyometers with scales and marks representing 100 feet per minute (ppm) are used. In the event that there is a failure in the static pressure takeover system, the variometer will be blocked at the last reading, or it may give erroneous readings in case of partial obstructions of the area or the shot.

87

In extreme cases, where the crew is reliably aware of the failure that occurs, breaking the instrument's glass will provide the device with the actual static pressure value. When it has a differential pressure again, the aneroid capsule will return with its expansion and expansion mechanics; a fact that will allow the instrument to give real values again.

Attitude indicator

The artificial horizon (or attitude indicator), is one of the essential flight instruments. This provides the pilot with pitching and balancing information, which is especially important when flying without external visual references. The attitude indicator works with a gyroscope that rotates in the horizontal plane. Therefore, it imitates the real horizon, through its rigidity in space. As the aircraft swings and rotates in relation to the real horizon, the gyroscope gimbals allow the aircraft and the instrument housing to swing and rotate around the gyroscope rotor that remains parallel to the ground. A horizontal representation of the miniature aircraft is fixed to the instrument housing.

A painted hemisphere that simulates the horizon, the sky and the ground, is attached to the gyroscopic gimbals. The sky and the ground meet in what is called the horizon bar. The relationship

88

between the horizon bar and the miniature plane is the same as that of the plane and the real horizon. The graduated scales refer to the degrees of pitching and balancing. Often, an adjustment knob allows pilots of different heights to place the horizon bar at an appropriate level.

Why does my plane fly?

We have reached one of the main unknowns of pilots when taking their first aeronautical steps. While there are different ways to give an accurate answer to this question, perhaps the simplest is to suppose that an airplane flies because it has a force that raises it due to an aerodynamic process that occurs in its wing profile.

Imagine we are standing in front of an open field and throwing a rock with all our strength. The rock will be flying, at least for a while, due to the force with which it was launched. Something similar happens with the plane, but continuously. Some forces act on it and enables you not only to stay in the air, but also to move through it.

Looking for a more technical answer to this initial question, we can assume that an aircraft can fly due to the action of four forces that exert an effect on its structure and generate a difference in

89

pressures between the bottom of the plane (wing) and the top of it, which enables the plane to rise and move through a certain space. To better understand this concept, we must study the four forces acting on an airplane. Let's see:

Forces Acting in Flight

When an aircraft is in flight, it is affected by a series of forces that can help the flight or reduce its capacity. There are four main forces that act constantly while an aircraft is in flight, they are:

These four forces act in pairs; the lift is opposite to weight, and thrust or traction, to resistance. An airplane or any other object remains static on the ground due to the action of two forces: its weight due to the gravity that keeps it on the ground and the inertia or resistance to advance that keeps it halted. For the plane to fly it would be necessary to counteract the effect of these two negative forces, weight and resistance, through two other positive forces in the opposite direction (Newton's Law), lift and thrust, respectively. In this way, the thrust can overcome the resistance that prevents the plane from moving forward, and the lift can exceed the weight of the plane by keeping it in the air. Let's see in detail each of these four forces:

Lift: It is the force developed by an aerodynamic profile moving in an air stream. It exerts its force from the bottom up and its direction is perpendicular to the relative wind, defined as the magnitude and direction of the air current lines with an opposite direction to the movement of the wing profile but "Not necessarily perpendicular to the horizon." It is represented with the letter L.

Weight: Weight is the gravitational attraction force on a body. Its direction is perpendicular to the surface of the earth and its sense is downwards and has an intensity proportional to the mass of that body. This force, opposed to support, is the one that pull the plane to the ground and keeps it there unless its opposite force takes action. Let's see:

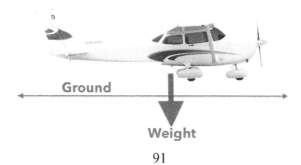

Thrust: To overcome the inertia of the stopped plane, as any object stopped on the surface, a "push" or "traction" force is necessary to generate a constant movement in the object to be able to move it, on the surface in the case of an object lacking support or through the air in the case of an airplane. This force is acquired by accelerating an air mass at a higher speed than that of the object or plane. The reaction, with an equal intensity but opposite direction (3rd Newton's law), moves the plane forward. In propeller planes, the propulsion force is generated by the rotation of the propeller, moved by the engine, and in reactors, propulsion is achieved by the violent expulsion of the gases burned by the turbine.

This tensile force is exerted in the same direction as the axis of the propellant system, which usually matches with the longitudinal axis of the aircraft. Let's see:

Thrust

Longitudinal Axis

The traction capacity of an aircraft is defined as "Power" and it depends on factors such as: the shape and size of the propeller, fuel octane, air density, etc. Tensile capacity or power is measured in horsepower (HP), conventional engines, and kilos or pounds of thrust in jet engines.

92

Drag: Drag is the force that prevents or slows the movement of an airplane. It acts in parallel and in the same direction as the relative wind. Let's see:

From an aerodynamic point of view, when a wing moves through the air, two types of resistances occur: on the one hand the resistance due to the friction of the air on the surface of the wing, and on the other hand, the resistance by the pressure of the air particle opposing the movement of an object.

Both resistances create a force proportional to the area on which they act and the square of the speed. Part of the pressure resistance, which produces a wing, depends on the amount of support it generates and is called "Induced Drag". The sum of the rest of the friction resistances on the rest of the surfaces is called "Parasitic Drag". Both will be a more detailed subject of study on the following pages.

Four Forces Interactions

Having met these four forces that act in our flight, let's see now in what condition each of these forces would act, since there will be a certain combination of force for each flight attitude.

- How do you think these four forces will be on a straight and level flight at constant speed? - Equal or unequal?

The correct answer is EQUAL! Since the four forces will exert the same pressure to keep the plane in flight an attitude of constant flight, i.e, without ascending or descending, and at a fixed speed, without accelerating or decelerating. Understanding this concept, we can say that in a level flight at a constant speed the lift is equal to weight and the traction is equal to the resistance: L=W (lift / weight) and T=D (thrust / drag).

Now, Let's see what would happen if any of the four forces alter its value and deviates from the remaining three. In the following example, traction alters its value and surmounts its opposite force, resistance . As a result of this variation of forces, there will be an acceleration, for the moment at constant altitude, since if it continues to increase its speed, so will the lift and the aircraft will begin to ascend.

94

- How do you think these forces will be in a normal situation after the takeoff of an aircraft?

Let's try to think about this question together. Immediately after taking off, an aircraft is in acceleration and continuous climb until the time comes for power reduction or altitude levelling. Considering this scenario, the forces would be represented as follows:

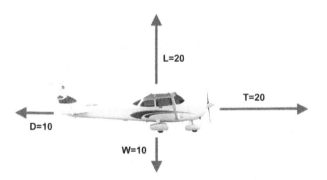

The lift would be greater than the weight (L > W) producing a climb and the traction would be greater than the resistance producing an acceleration (T > D).

95

Airfoil

An aerodynamic profile or airfoil is considered the backbone of an airplane and keeps in itself the secret of the flight. Imagine that we take the wing of an airplane and manage to remove its coverage, in there we will find a large number of profiles side by side forming the wing structure, just as each rib in the human skeleton. Let's see:

The sum of a certain number of "ribs" or profiles within the structure of a wing, will define its size. In this second image we see a complete wing, with all its profiles joined by the beams or internal beams in the wing that unify each profile forming the complete structure of the wing.

Now, having understood this concept, let's go on to detail the most important parts of an airfoil and then understand its principle of operation.

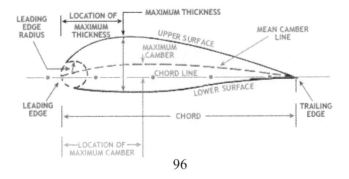

96

Leading Edge: Curved and frontal section of the airfoil where the path of the air particles begins when impacting the surface of the wing. It is the direct impact zone with the air stream, its shape and size define the  potential of the air particle to travel the wing surface and generate lift. If for some reason, for example ice formation, the leading edge is distorted, it would make it difficult for the air particle to travel, affecting the lift to the point where the particle would be unable to pass the deformity and the aircraft could enter into loss.

Trailing Edge: Final section of the wing surface where the air flow returns to the free current after having travelled the entire surface of the profile. This section has the particularity of being able to extend and enlarge the wing surface by means of high lift devices such as FLAPS.

Lower Surface: Bottom of the wing that covers from the leading edge to the trailing edge.

Upper Surface: Top of the wing that covers from the leading edge to the starting edge.

Maximum Thickness: Maximum distance between the lower and upper surfaces. There can only be a maximum thickness for each profile.

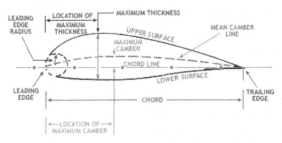

Chord: It is an imaginary straight line that joins the leading and exit edges. It is crucial since, along with the relative wind, it is one of the two variables to take into account for the calculation of the angle of attack. On an other note, the rope defines the size of the profile since in a wing there can be profiles of different sizes in order to reduce the size of the wing tips and thus obtain an aerodynamic benefit.

Flow Around the Airfoil

Speed distribution around the airfoil: When a profile moves through the air, variations occur in the speed of the air along its surface.

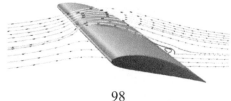

The current lines on the upper and upper surfaces of an airfoil come together when crossing the aerodynamic profile. Similar to the Venturi effect, this phenomenon occurs when the velocity of free current increases. This increase in velocity is due to the fact that the draft must be split to let the profile pass. Some of the air flows above the profile and some, below it, but the current lines must be joined at the leaking edge of the airfoil to re-form the air stream free of disturbances.

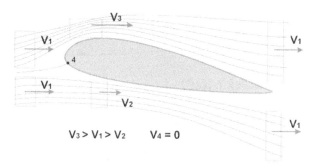

Due to the upper curvature of the profile, the air that passes over the upper surface (Upper Surface) has a greater distance to travel to reach the leakage edge than the distance that the air particle that passes under the profile (Lower Surface) must travel. Considering that the particles move in the same free-air current line, both must reach the leaking edge at the same time, so particles that have a longer distance to travel must do so at a higher speed to maintain the time value constant. This is how the velocity of air flow around a profile acts.

Let's apply this concept to the wing of an airplane and see how the aforementioned effect occurs on the wing profile, or in this case on the entire surface of the plane formed by a series of ordered profiles. The entire plane of the aircraft is introduced into the outdoor current modifying the path of its particles through the surfaces of the upper and lower surfaces.

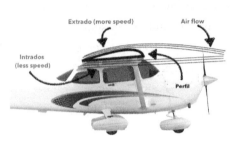

Angle of Attack (AOA)

We will take as an example the traditional flat profile. One of the most important points to take into account when talking about profiles is the well-known "Attack Angle" or AOA (angle of attack), which is formed by the direction of the outdoor current or relative wind and the aerodynamic rope of our profile.

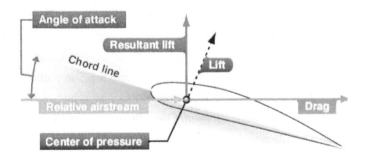

100

This angle is variable, since it depends on the direction of the relative wind and the position of the wings with respect to it, both points controlled by the pilot. It is important to know that the angle of attack is measured with respect to the relative wind and the aerodynamic rope, but not in relation to the horizon line and the longitudinal axis of the plane, variables that are usually easily confused.

On an other note, we find the "Angle of Incidence (AOI)", formed by the aerodynamic chord and the longitudinal axis of the plane. This is a fixed angle and is defined by the manufacturer of each aircraft. Let's see:

In short, in a profile we can find two different types of angles. On the one hand, the angle of attack or AOA, formed by the aerodynamic rope and the relative wind, an angle at which the pilot can take action to modify the lift and resistance values. On the other hand, there is the angle of incidence AOI, formed by the aerodynamic rope and the longitudinal axis of the aircraft. Defined by the manufacturer and of a fixed value, wich can´t be modified by the pilot's actions. Let's see a practical example of these two angles in the following graph:

Having understood the difference between these two angles, we will stop to analyse the effect of the angle of attack on the lift. This variable can pose a risk to the flight. While it manages to have control over the lift, an excessive angle of attack could generate a complete loss of lift. The effect of increasing the angle of attack is similar to increasing the curvature of the upper part of the profile, that is, the narrowing to the air flow and, therefore, the difference in pressures and, consequently, the lift. The relationship between the lift and the angle of attack gives as a result a maximum lift coefficient called CL MAX. Let's look at the following graph to better understand this concept

In this figure it is seen, in general, how the sustain coefficient (CL) increases with the angle of attack until it reaches the maximum CL, from which the lift decreases with the angle of attack until it reaches the complete loss of it, a situation known as "Sustainable Loss" or "STALL".

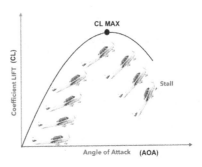

Chapter 3

The sky

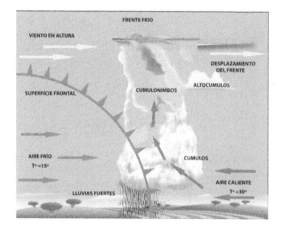

The Temperature

Formally, the temperature is a magnitude related to the speed of movement of the particles that make up matter. The greater the disturbance they present, the higher the temperature. In meteorology, it is common to talk about maximum and minimum temperatures, the highest and lowest values recorded in a period, for example, one day. Two thermometric scales commonly known as Celsius (centigrades) and Fahrenheit are used to measure these temperatures.

The Celsius scale °C consists of a regular division into 100 intervals, where 0 corresponds to the freezing point of the water and 100 to its boiling point. It is expressed in degrees Celsius and is the one we usually use. The Fahrenheit °F scale is commonly used in the United States. The thermometer is graduated between 32°F (corresponding to 0"C) and 212°F (corresponding to 100°C).

Looking for a simple definition of atmospheric temperature, we can say that it is one of the elements that make up the climate.

Indicates the amount of heat energy accumulated in the air at a certain time and place. It comes from the rays emitted by the sun, that is, solar radiation that reaches the earth. These rays are reflected by the Earth's surface and sent back into space. Thanks to the atmosphere, the sun's rays return to the earth, allowing the heat to stay longer and causing the greenhouse effect.

The atmosphere is made up of gases. Thanks to them, our planet has an average temperature, one of which is CO2. But if these gases are very abundant, the atmosphere becomes thicker, causing the sun's rays to be on earth for longer. Staying there and continuing to receive rays of sunshine, there is a greater increase in the temperature of the earth. Therefore, the more gases are in the atmosphere, the higher the temperature, since it will prevent the heat from leaving into space. The temperature variation, contrary to what one might think, does not decrease as height is acquired in the atmosphere. In the troposphere it decreases steadily with altitude, at a rate of about 6.4°C per 1000 meters. This is called the vertical temperature gradient. When you reach the height of 14 kilometers, where the limit of this layer or tropopause is located, the temperature stops falling sharply and increases. Already in the stratosphere, the temperature increases to 0°C when it reaches 50 kilometers high, where stratopause is located. From here begins the mesosphere, where the temperature drops again to -80°C until it reaches the mesopause. From here begins the thermosphere, where the temperature rises again.

The Dew Point

Furthermore, hand in hand with temperature, we find the "Dew Point". We can define it as the value to which the air temperature must drop so that the existing steam begins to condense. The dew point can be calculated directly with the temperature and

106

relative humidity data existing at any given time. These data can come from meteorological reports broadcast radially, or recorded by instruments, but to make it simpler we will learn to use a simple table to easily calculate the "dew point". Let's see an example and use the table on the following page:

If on a given day, in the city we have 26° temperature and 60% relative humidity, the corresponding dew point (according to the table) is 18°. But what do these 18 degrees mean? Simple, if the air in the area cools quickly, and the temperature drops from the current 26° to the 18° of the "dew point", two consecutive weather phenomena will happen. First, very small drops of liquid water (dew) will form on all smooth surfaces that are outdoors. Those droplets of dew are the ones that give the name to our "dew point". Immediately, water condensation will also occur in the air, forming countless droplets of suspended water, which constitute a fog.

TEMPERATURAS (en grados C)	Humedad relativa																
	20%	25%	30%	35%	40%	45%	50%	55%	60%	65%	70%	75%	80%	85%	90%	95%	100%
40°	13	16	19	21	24	26	28										
39°	13	15	18	20	23	25	27	28									
38°	12	14	17	20	22	24	26	27									
37°	11	13	16	19	21	23	25	26	28								
36°	10	12	15	18	20	22	24	25	27	28							
35°	9	11	15	17	19	21	23	24	26	27	28						
34°	8	10	14	16	18	20	22	23	25	26	27	28					
33°	7	10	13	15	17	19	21	22	24	25	26	27	28				
32°	6	9	12	14	16	18	20	21	23	24	25	26	27	28			
31°	5	8	11	13	15	17	19	20	22	23	24	25	26	27			
30°	4	7	10	12	15	17	18	20	21	22	23	25	26	27	28		
29°	4	6	9	11	14	16	17	19	20	21	22	24	25	26	27	28	
28°	3	5	8	10	13	15	17	18	20	20	21	23	24	25	26	27	28
27°	2	4	7	9	12	14	16	17	19	20	20	22	23	24	25	26	27
26°	1	3	6	8	11	13	15	16	18	19	20	21	22	23	24	25	26
25°	1	3	6	8	10	12	14	15	17	18	19	20	21	22	23	24	25
24°	0	2	5	7	9	11	13	14	16	17	18	19	20	21	22	23	24
23°	0	1	4	6	8	10	12	13	14	16	17	18	19	20	21	22	23
22°	-1	1	3	5	7	9	11	12	13	15	16	17	18	19	20	21	22
21°	-2	0	2	5	6	8	10	11	12	14	15	16	17	18	19	20	21
20°	-3	-1	2	4	6	7	9	10	11	13	14	15	16	17	18	19	20

Observing in a meteorological report known as METAR (theme to be studied in subsequent chapters), this information could be found as follows: 5000 FG 18/18, with 5000 being the reduced visibility value by fog or FOG (FG), a phenomenon that is formed when the temperature and the dew point come together as in this example where it appears 18/18.

Atmospheric Pressure

The air around us, even if we don't notice it, weighs, and therefore exerts a force on all bodies due to the action of gravity. This force per unit surface is called atmospheric pressure and its unit of measurement in the International System is Pascal. Atmospheric pressure depends on many variables, especially altitude. The higher in the atmosphere we find ourselves, the lower the amount of air above us will be, which will also reduce the pressure it exerts on a body located there. The following graph shows the averagevalues of atmospheric pressure as a function of altitude. In it we can see how atmospheric pressure drops with height.

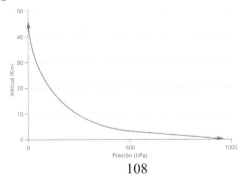

The atmospheric pressure varies, it is not always the same in different parts of our planet and our country, nor at different times of year. To measure pressure we have the help of a device called Barometer, invented by the Italian physicist called Evangelista Torricelli in 1643. In meteorology, the Hectopascal (HPA) is used as a unit of measurement of atmospheric pressure. The normal pressure, usually called "standard", above sea level is 1013.2 HPA.

Pressure and altimetry

Considering altimetry as the technique of measuring vertical distances, we find that it is directly affected by atmospheric pressure. The tool to carry out this technique is the Barometer, which in aviation is commonly called "Altimeter", instead of measuring units of pressure, measures height increases, which can be "True" or "Indicated", being the true one, that with reference to sea level, and the indicated, that with reference to a certain area having adjusted the adjustment of the altimeter to the local value.

Pressure and instability or atmospheric stability

The air has a very simple dynamic and is related to its density and temperature. The hottest air is less dense and the colder is denser. That's why, when the air is colder it tends to drop in altitude and the opposite when it is warmer. This air dynamic causes changes in atmospheric pressure causing instability or stability in the environment.

Stability or Anticyclone (high pressure)

When the air is colder and descends, it increases the atmospheric pressure since there is more air on the surface and therefore exerts more force. This causes atmospheric stability also called anticyclone. This situation is characterized by being an area of calm, without winds since the coldest and heaviest air is slowly descending in a circular direction. The air rotates almost imperceptibly clockwise in the northern hemisphere and anti-clockwise in the southern hemisphere.

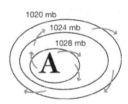

Instability or Cyclone (low pressure)

On the contrary, when hot air rises, it lowers atmospheric pressure and causes instability called cyclone or storm. The wind always moves in the preferred direction to those areas with lower atmospheric pressure, that is, whenever an area has a cyclone, the wind will be greater, because being an area of lower pressure, the wind will go there.

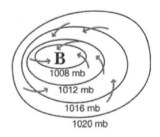

When cold air and hot air are on the surface, cold air pushes hot air upwards causing decreases in pressures and instability. A cyclone is then formed in the contact area between hot and cold air. This phenomenon is called front and is divided into two groups: Cold Fronts and Warm Fronts. Let's see:

Cold fronts

On these fronts the mass of cold air replaces the hot one. They are strong and can cause atmospheric disturbances such as storms, tornadoes, strong winds and short snowstorms before the passage of the cold front.

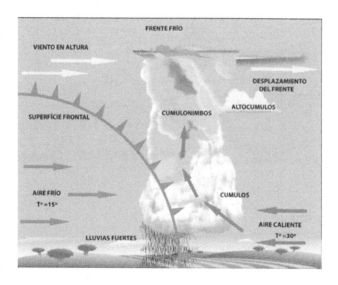

Warm fronts

Warm fronts are those in which a mass of hot air gradually replaces cold air. Generally, with the passage of the warm front the temperature and humidity increase, the pressure drops and although the wind changes, it is not as pronounced as when a cold front passes. Precipitation in the form of rain, snow or drizzle is usually found at the beginning of a surface front.

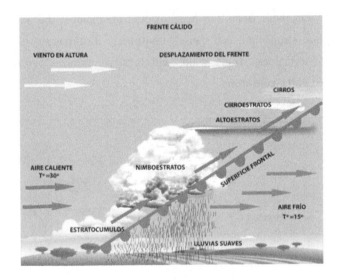

The wind

This phenomenon consists of the movement of air from one area to another. There are several causes that can create the existence of wind, but it usually originates when a certain difference in pressure or temperature is established between two points.

112

In the first case, when between two zones the air pressure is different, it tends to move from the high pressure zone to the low pressure zone. Something similar to what happens inside a toothpaste tube when we press at one end to bring out the toothpaste. When tightening, what we produce is a difference in pressure between that point and the open end. Meteorologists would say that there has been a gradient or pressure difference between the two extremes.

In the atmosphere, there is a direct relationship between pressure and wind, which means that isobar maps, which represent the values of atmospheric pressure, contain extensive information about the speed and direction of the wind. You just need to know how to interpret them! We will study these maps in the following chapter.

In the event that the origin of the wind is a thermal difference, what happens is that when an air mass acquires a higher temperature than its environment, its volume increases, which decreases its density. Due to flotation, the mass of hot air will ascend, and its place will be occupied by other air masses, which in their displacement will cause the wind.

Different equipment is used to be able to measure the direction and intensity of the wind. Let's see:

On the one hand, we have the "Intensity Measurement": the most used instrument is the anemometer of cups or windlasses (figure A) in which the rotation of them is proportional to the wind speed. The unit of measurement is usually km/h or KTs.

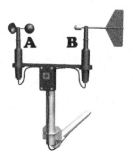

On the other hand, we have the "Direction Measure": for this purpose the weather vanes are used (figure B), which indicate the geographical origin of the wind.

In aviation, wind measurement is given in Knots per hour and the direction always corresponds to the sector from which it comes but based on 360°. This means that a reported wind of 360 degrees with 10 knots, being 360/10, runs from North to South and its intensity is 10 Knots.

We know that all objects that float in the atmosphere and with this we include aircraft, are affected in the same way by the wind. Imagine momentarily that we release a balloon with helium, when ascending it will have a vertical and a horizontal movement that will depend on the wind conditions. If it blows from the north with a speed of 10 knots, the balloon will move and in an hour it would be 10 nautical miles south from place where it was released.

In the same way, the flight of an airplane is affected, with the difference that it has its own movement force, which will always be affected by the wind component regardless of the size or weight of

114

the aircraft, the difference will be the speed with which it moves and therefore the time the wind affects its movement.

The surface wind

At a great height of the ground surface, about a kilometer, the land surface hardly exerts any influence on the wind. However, in the lower layers of the atmosphere, wind speeds are affected by friction with the Earth's surface. This causes the higher the height, the faster the wind speed, although this increase in speed is very pronounced in the first meters. The terrain affects the wind on the surface, perhaps the most pronounced is the effect of the orography. Since air movements in the atmosphere are limited in the lower layers by the "troposphere", the mountains decrease the section through which the wind can circulate. As the air cannot disappear or compress, a consequence of this decrease in section and conservation of the mass is the increase in speed ("Venturi effect"). Let's see the following graph:

Basic Reading of the Wind

There are different reports that will inform the pilot about the direction and intensity of the wind. One of the most well-known are the so- called "Arrows or Wind Lines". In these arrows with barbs,

115

the wind speed is represented taking into account the following graphic scale. The smaller barb equals 5 knots, the largest barb 10 knots and the triangle 50 knots; if we want to represent 70 knots it will be a triangle with two large barbs. Speeds below 5 knots are represented with arrows without barbs. Let's look at the scale and some examples:

●	Calm	●—⟍	20 kt
●—⟋	5 kt	●—◣	50 kt
●—⟍	10 kt	●—⟍⟍	65 kt
●—⟍⟍	15 kt		

In this example, the wind information is as follows: wind from 120° at

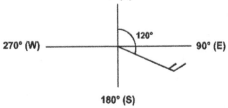

In aviation we have certain visual references that give us information about wind direction and intensity. The best known is the windsock, located within an aerodrome and near the runway. This system is based on a windsock resting on a rotor, which allows a rotation at 360' to indicate its direction.

116

In terms of intensity, the windsock has five sections of white and red colors. Starting from the root, the first section indicates 3 KT of intensity, the second 6 KT, and so on from to 3 KT up to a maximum of 15 knots of intensity. Let's see:

The HA windsock windspeed guide

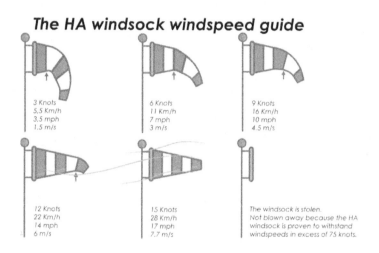

The Clouds

This important meteorological phenomenon is of vital importance for each pilot, who should be able to look at the sky and identify what kinds of clouds he is observing. In the following pages, we will try to give you the tools to achieve this goal. Let's start by trying to define the term "Cloud":

We can say that a cloud is the physical and visual materialization of atmospheric water vapor that, when changing phases (liquid or solid) and grouping, forms structures that cover all or partially the sky. The interaction of sunlight with droplets and ice crystallites makes clouds appear, preferably white, other times they are grayish and even black at sight. The sun's rays at sunrise and sunset adorn the clouds with various characteristic colors.

The differences between cloud formations are due, in part, to the different condensation temperatures. When it occurs at temperatures below freezing, clouds are usually formed by ice crystals; however, those that formed in warmer air usually contain droplets of water.

The air movement associated with the creation of clouds also affects their formation. Clouds that are created in resting air tend to appear in layers or strata, while those that form between winds or air with strong vertical currents have a great vertical development.

Considering that the troposphere is divided into three layers at different heights, we can classify the clouds according to the layer they occupy.

Clouds near the ground and reaching up to 3 km high are called Low Clouds. Those that occupy an intermediate level between 3 and 7 km will be the Middle Clouds. The High Clouds are those that occupy the upper level of the troposphere and can reach up to 14 km in height or more.

Finally, we find a special case, vertical development clouds formed by cloudy systems that extend from low to very high layers, known as "Cumulonimbus". Another classification is according to its shape.

The English scientist Luke Howard called the bulging clouds, which appear as piled up, cumulus, which in Latin means heap. Layered clouds were called stratus, which means layer or veil. The ones shaped as a strand of hair were called cirrus and the heavy with rain ones, he called them nimbus.

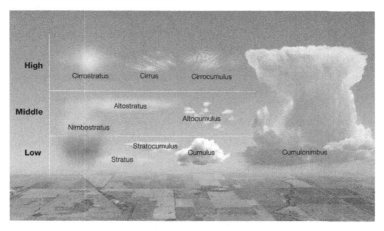

Let's start by getting to know each of them to be able to identify them with at a glance.

Cirrus (Ci). Cirros. High Cloud

They are presented as separate clouds in the form of delicate white filaments. They have a fibrous appearance, similar to a person's hair. Formed by tiny ice crystals, as they form at high altitude (8-12Km.). At these levels the temperature ranges from -40 °C to -60°C, so a mass of air, with a high water vapor content and that cools to saturation, produces ice crystals instead of droplets of water. Its presence indicates strong winds at higher levels. When they are isolated they are symptomatic of good weather, but if they advance organized and progressively increasing towards the horizon they indicate an imminent weather change or the presence of some front.

Cirrostratus (Cs). Cirrostratos. High Cloud

Cloudy, transparent and whitish veil, fibrous (like hair) or completely smooth appearance, which covers all or part of the sky. They are made up of very fine ice crystals, even more so than those of the Cirrus. They form when a large-scale wet air mass rises to high altitudes until sublimated. These clouds occupy vast expanses of the sky, at an altitude of between 7-10 km.

Usually, due to its extreme finesse, it becomes difficult to distinguish whether the sky is covered or clear. Cirrostratus are usually the vanguard of a Warm Front, increasing their thickness as it progresses, so their presence can be associated with a significant weather change.

Cirrocumulus (Cc). Cirrocúmulos. High Cloud

We can describe them as a bank, thin layer or layer of white clouds, without shadows, composed of very small elements in the form of grains, curls, lumps, undulations, joined or separated and distributed more or less regularly. Made up of ice crystals, they have a formation process similar to Ci and Cs. Unlike the Ci and Cs, the Cirrocumulus inform on the presence of instability at the level at which they are, and that gives these clouds their cumuliform appearance. They are located at heights of 7-12Km. Unless they increase considerably over time, they usually do not indicate a weather change.

Due to their appearance, these cloudy formations are easy to confuse with Altocumulus, of similar appearance but lower, gray and with larger constituent elements.

Altocúmulus (Ac). Altocúmulos. Middle Cloud

Bank, thin layer or layer of white or gray clouds, or white and gray at the same time, which have shadows composed of rounded masses, rollers, etc., which are sometimes partially fibrous or diffuse and may or may not be joined. Normally consisting of tiny drops of water. When the temperature is very low, ice crystals form. They form when a large mass of air, pushed by a frontal system, ascends to the average levels, (4-6Km.) and subsequently condensing. In turn, these clouds are formed by unstable air masses, which gives them their cumuliform appearance. They are usually part of cold fronts and warm fronts.

123

Altostratus (As). Altostratos. Middle Cloud

Sheet or layer of clouds, grayish or bluish, fluted, fibrous or uniform in appearance, covering the sky entirely or partially, like a large sheet. It has parts thin enough to vaguely distinguish the Sun, as through a tarnished glass. Consisting of an upper area composed of ice crystals. A half part mixture of ice crystals, snow crystals or flakes and droplets of overcooled water. And a lower part, composed entirely of droplets of water overcooled. It is the cloud that occupies the largest tracts of land. It also forms the middle and lower part of the anvil of a Cumulonimbus. It is usually found between 3 and 7 km high, and its thickness can vary between 1 and 4 km. This family of clouds is associated with warm fronts and usually gives continuous rain or weak snowfall.

Nimbostratus (Ns). Nimbostratos. Middle Cloud

Layer of gray clouds, often dark, with an appearance veiled by the precipitation of rain or snow that falls more or less continuously from it. The thickness of the cloud is large enough to hide the Sun completely. Composed of tiny drops of water, raindrops over cool, crystals and snowflakes. Nimbostratus is usually formed by ascending a huge and extensive layer of relatively warm and humid air above a cold mass, in a progressive and gentle slope. It is, along with the Ace, the main nucleus of a warm front. It is a very difficult cloud to distinguish, since it is presented as a uniform dark gray veil, without any discontinuity and occupying the entire sky, mixed with precipitation. Likewise, it occupies a large vertical dimension, in the thickest sites, it can cover between 1- 5 km.

Stratus (St). Estratos. Low Cloud

Layer of generally gray clouds, with a uniform base, from which drizzle can fall. When the sun is visible through the layer, its outline is clearly distinguished. It is composed of tiny drops of water. At very low temperatures it can consist of small ice particles. They are usually between 0 and 300 m. of the ground. Its formation is due to the combined effect of cooling in the lower layers of the atmosphere and turbulence due to wind. They form on the ground, by night irradiation or by advection of relatively warm air on colder soil. Over the sea, cooling is usually by advection. They produce fog if they are at the surface level.

Stratocumulus (Sc). Estratocúmulos. Low Cloud

Bank, sheet or layer of gray or whitish clouds, which almost always have dark parts; composed of rounded masses and rollers that are joined or not. It is the most common type of cloud. They can be formed within a mass of humid air in low layers, occupying a large extension, or also by an inversion of temperature that forces the Cu, in vertical development, to stop their ascent and extend in the form of Sc. In the first case they usually form between 500 m and 2 km high, and in the second between 2-3 km. They are associated with good weather when in summer they appear mid-afternoon as a result of the evolution of the Cu of good weather. They also usually appear associated with Warm or Cold Fronts mixed with a large layer of As/Ns.

127

Cumulus (Cu). Cúmulos.Vertical grow Cloud

Isolated clouds, generally dense and with well-defined contours, develop vertically in the form of bumps, domes or towers, and whose convex upper parts often resemble a cauliflower. The parts of these Sunlit clouds are bright white; their base is dark and horizontal. Sometimes, they appear torn by the wind. They develop when convective currents occur caused by the unequal warming of air on the Earth's surface. This air when ascending condenses into a cloud form and will grow depending on the degree of instability of the air existing at that time. Good weather Cu grows in summer from noon to sunset, when they dissipate. If there is a certain degree of instability, they can progress to Cu Congestus and, where appropriate, become Cumulonimbus, with showers and storms.

Cumulonimbus (Cb). Cumulonimbos. Vertical grow Cloud

Irregular and dense clouds, with considerable vertical development, in the form of a mountain or huge towers. Part, at least, of its top is normally smooth or crushed; this part often extends in the form of an anvil. Below the base, torn low clouds and precipitation appear. Consisting of tiny drops of water and ice crystals on top. Inside they contain large raindrops, snowflakes, granulated ice and hail. They originate mainly in spring and summer in situations of instability. They have great vertical development. The stops are usually between 8 and 14 km high. They almost always produce storms, that is, intense rainfall, rain or hail, but also snow in winter, accompanied by winds and electric shocks that occur between clouds or between cloud and land (lightning).

Turbulence

Everyone who flies encounters turbulence at some time or other. A turbulent atmosphere is one in which air currents vary greatly over short distances. These currents range from rather mild eddies to strong currents of relatively large dimensions. As an aircraft moves through these currents, it undergoes changing accelerations which jostle it from its smooth flight path. This jostling is turbulence. Turbulence ranges from bumpiness which can annoy crew and passengers to severe jolts which can structurally damage the aircraft or injure its passengers.

Aircraft reaction to turbulence varies with the difference in windspeed in adjacent currents, size of the aircraft, wing loading, airspeed, and aircraft attitude. When an aircraft travels rapidly from one current to another, it undergoes abrupt changes in acceleration. Obviously, if the aircraft moved more slowly, the changes in acceleration would be more gradual. The first rule in flying turbulence is to reduce airspeed. Your aircraft manual most likely lists recommended airspeed for penetrating turbulence.

The expression turbulence is generally taken to refer to disturbed or rough air whose movement is of a disordered, swirling nature, causing air to move out of its immediate environment and mix with other layers of air. Turbulence will have an effect on an

130

aircraft's in-flight attitude, but will generally allow the aircraft to maintain its flight path.

Quantitative indications of turbulence intensity can be determined from the onboard measurements of g-load, airspeed fluctuations, and rate-of-climb. G-load (or gust load) is the force that arises because of the influence of gravity. Normal gravity corresponds to a g-load of 1.0g. A change in g-load above or below the normal value is a rough measure of the intensity of the turbulence. For example, if an aircraft experiences a total g-load of +1.5g, it means that associated turbulence (or maneuvering) caused an excess load of +0.5g.

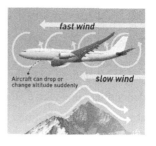

Airspeed fluctuations refer to the largest positive and negative airspeed deviations from the average during a turbulent event. For example, if your average airspeed is 140 knots with variations between 130 and 150 knots, you are experiencing fluctuations of ± 10 knots. Rate of climb simply refers to the largest positive or negative values during horizontal flight through a turbulent region.

	Airspeed Fluctuation (kts)	Change in G-load (g)	Vertical Gust (f.p.m.)
Light	5 – 14.9	0.20 – 0.49	300 – 1199
Moderate	15 – 24.9	0.50 – 0.99	1200 – 2099
Severe	≥25	1.0 – 1.99	2100 – 2999
Extreme	—	≥2.00	≥3000

131

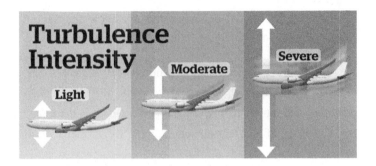

Types of turbulence

Aviation turbulence can be divided into four categories, depending on where the turbulence occurs, what larger scale atmospheric circulations are present, and what is producing the turbulence. The categories are low-level turbulence (LLT), turbulence in and near thunderstorms (TNT), clear-air turbulence (CAT), and mountain wave turbulence (MWT).

Low Level Turbulence LLT

One of the most common causes of low level turbulence is disturbance of the air as it flows over irregularly shaped surfaces, such as hills, buildings, trees etc.

The layer of air in which this type of disturbance is likely to take place is known as the friction layer. Above the friction layer, the flow of air is unaffected by the surface. The upper boundary of the friction layer is called the friction level.

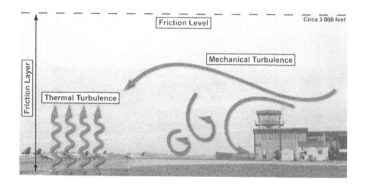

Turbulence caused by air flow disturbed by surface features is called mechanical turbulence. The depth of the friction layer will be influenced by the extent of mechanical interference from trees and buildings.

Over flat ground, significant LLT occurs when surface winds are strong. This is called mechanical turbulence. It occurs because friction slows the wind in the lowest layers causing the air to turn over in turbulent eddies.

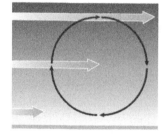

Turbulencia alrededor de tormentas TNT

Turbulence in and near thunderstorms (TNT) is that turbulence which occurs within developing convective clouds and

133

thunderstorms, in the vicinity of thunderstorm tops and wakes, in downbursts, and in gust fronts.

Turbulence near thunderstorms (TNT) occurs in three different turbulence regions: within thunderstorms, under thunderstorms and around and over thunderstorms.

Turbulence within storms: Turbulence is also found in and around significant cloud developments, especially in cumuliform cloud, which are convective clouds created by rising air currents.

The vertical extent of a cumulus cloud is therefore a very good indication of the intensity of the vertical air flow beneath and within the cloud, and, consequently, the intensity of the turbulence in and around the cloud. For this reason, pilots must treat large cumuliform clouds with caution. Cumulonimbus clouds generate the most violent turbulence. In cumulonimbus clouds, and well developed cumulus cloud, both up-currents and downdraughts are present within the cloud, itself.

Turbulence inside thunderstorms occurs on at least two different scales. The largest eddies have sizes comparable to the major updrafts and downdrafts. Small scale gusts are produced by strong shears on the edges of the vertical drafts.

In the cumulus stage of thunderstorm development, the turbulence inside the storm is due to the updraft, which usually occupies less than half the cloud volume. Updraft speeds increase from the base of the cloud to a maximum near the top of the cloud.

In the mature stage, updraft speeds accelerate through the depth of the storm, reaching a maximum in the upper part of the cell at the equilibrium level. This is often (but not always) near the tropopause. Because of the rapid rate of rise of the cloud tops, pilots flying just below the tropopause are occasionally surprised with a strong burst of turbulence as the top of a growing cumulonimbus cloud reaches flight level.

Turbulence intensity increases with the development of the thunderstorm; that is, light and moderate intensities in the cumulus stage and moderate and severe (or worse) in the mature stage. When the thunderstorm cell begins to dissipate, turbulence within the thunderstorm weakens. However, a high degree of caution should be exercised in the visual evaluation of turbulence potential. For example, early in the dissipating stage, turbulence in some locations of the thunderstorm is as intense as it is in the mature stage. Late in the dissipating stage, isolated patches of severe turbulence may still be present. Also, in multicell thunderstorms, a nearby, mature cell may be obscured by the clouds of a dissipating cell.

Turbulence around storms: Around well developed cumulus cloud, (cumulus congestus), and cumulonimbus, downdraughts are active at some distance from the cloud itself. These downdraughts cause severe turbulence.

Turbulence "around the thunderstorm" refers to that found outside the main region of convection. This includes turbulence in clear and cloudy air next to the main cumulonimbus cloud and turbulence in and over the anvil cloud.

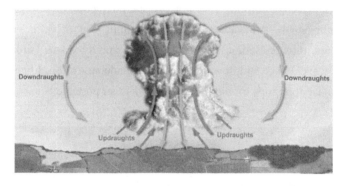

Turbulence is produced outside the thunderstorm when the cell acts as a barrier to the large scale airflow. Multicell and supercell thunderstorms move more slowly than the winds at upper levels. Under these conditions, part of the prevailing airflow is diverted around the thunderstorm, producing a variety of turbulent eddies. This effect is greater with strong thunderstorms and with strong winds aloft.

137

A turbulent wake occurs under the anvil cloud downwind of the thunderstorm. This is one of the most hazardous regions outside of the thunderstorm and above its base. Sometimes referred to as the "region under the overhang (anvil)," it is well known to experienced pilots as the location of severe turbulence and, possibly, hail.

Near the top of the thunderstorm, several circulations are possible. The cumuliform appearance of the overshooting tops is a warning that this region is a source of significant turbulence due to the convective currents. Additionally, the interaction of strong winds in the stable stratosphere with the updraft can produce vertical shears, turbulent eddies, and atmospheric gravity waves (similar to lee waves) over and downwind of the thunderstorm top. Flight near thunderstorm tops should be avoided wherever possible.

Turbulence under storms: Beneath the base of cumulus congestus and cumulonimbus, convective upcurrents are also very strong. Downdraughts can be met beneath the cloud base, too. The most severe downdraughts occur in precipitation. When precipitation falls from clouds, it tends to drag air down with it, creating downdraughts within, and underneath the cloud.

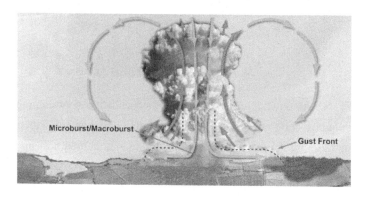

The downdrafts, downbursts, and microbursts define the primary turbulent areas below the thunderstorm. These phenomena produce intense turbulence as well as wind shear. Strong winds in the outflow from the downdraft generate mechanical turbulence, which is especially strong along the edge of any microburst and/or gust front.

Of course, extreme turbulence is also to be expected near any funnel clouds, tornadoes, and other tornado-like vortices. The combination of turbulence and wind shear with heavy precipitation, low ceilings, and poor visibilities makes the area below a thunderstorm very dangerous.

139

If the downdraught descends from beneath a cumulonimbus or cumulus congestus, it will usually come into contact with the ground, and then spread out from the cloud, sometimes up to distances from the cloud of 15 - 20 miles. This type of phenomenon causes large changes in the direction and speed of the wind in the vicinity of the cloud, both vertically and horizontally, and may thus give rise to dangerous low level windshear.

Clear Air Turbulence CAT

Clear air turbulence (CAT) is that turbulence which occurs in the free atmosphere away from any visible convective activity. CAT includes high level frontal and jet stream turbulence, typically above 15,000 feet MSL. Its name is derived from early experiences of pilots who encountered significant high-level turbulence in clear skies; however, we now know that the processes that produce CAT can also be present in clouds. Nevertheless, the name remains "CAT."

140

Because we can't observe CAT very well, we often find it more convenient to describe it in statistical terms. For example, during a given flight anywhere in the atmosphere, an aircraft has about a 6 in 100 (6%) chance of encountering moderate or greater CAT. The chance of severe or greater CAT is less than 1 percent. The chances of encountering CAT are usually higher in regions near the jet stream. A 10% probability of encountering moderate or greater CAT is considered large. Therefore, keep in mind as we discuss "favored" areas and "higher" frequencies for CAT that these are relative terms. On an absolute scale, the chances of moderate or greater CAT are almost always small.

This turbulence is found near high level stable layers that have vertical wind shear. When air parcels in a stable layer are displaced vertically, atmospheric gravity waves develop. These waves can have wavelengths from a few hundred feet to a mile or two. If the vertical shear is strong, it causes the wave crests to overrun the wave troughs, creating a very unstable situation. The air literally "overturns" in the waves, often violently.

The result is a layer of CAT. Known as shearing-gravity waves, they are often superimposed on much longer mountain lee waves.

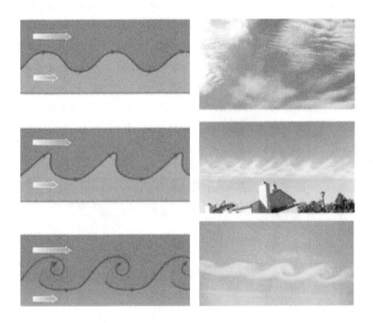

CAT occurs more frequently within a few thousand feet of the tropopause, over mountains, and in winter. CAT tends to occur in thin layers, typically less than 2,000 feet deep, a few tens of miles wide and more than 50 miles long. CAT often occurs in sudden bursts as aircraft intersect thin, sloping turbulent layers.

CAT forecasting has always been difficult because of the lack of good observations at the microscale where CAT occurs. Usually, the exact locations of CAT cannot be specified unless an aircraft

142

happens to encounter and report the turbulence. In the past, forecasts were made primarily on the basis of PIREPs and known statistical relationships between CAT occurrences and large scale weather patterns.

Mountain Wave turbulence MWT

As stable air flows over a hill or mountain, it begins to oscillate in a wave-like pattern. The crests of these oscillations are known, generally, as mountain waves, lee waves, or standing waves. Mountain waves can reach high up into the atmosphere, creating disturbances which reach well into the Stratosphere. Mountain waves are generally stationary, with the oscillating air molecules maintaining their mean position, hence the term standing wave. The creation of mountain waves requires specific atmospheric conditions to prevail.

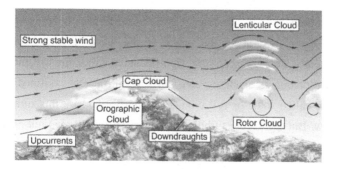

Firstly, the air must be very stable, otherwise the air flow, when reaching the mountain, would simply rise vertically, and the oscillation pattern would not establish itself. Also, the wind speed at the level of the mountain's ridge must be of sufficiently high speed, and this speed must increase with altitude. A further crucial factor is the direction of the wind in relation to the orientation of the range of mountains or hills. The wind direction must be roughly across the range of hills or mountains.

Often, mountain waves may become visible, because they can create very distinctive cloud formations. As the air rises, in the up-going part of the oscillation associated with mountain wave, it will cool adiabatically. This adiabatic cooling may cause condensation to take place, and cloud to form. However, when air descends during the second half of the oscillation, it will be compressed and warm up, causing the newly formed cloud to evaporate. Cloud formed in this way takes on a lens-like shape. This is the reason why mountain wave clouds are called altocumulus lenticularis or, more commonly, lenticular cloud.

Although the flow of air within mountain waves is laminar and smooth, severe turbulence may be present beneath the wave. The flow of air underneath the peaks of the waves is often rotating turbulently. This zone can pose significant danger to aircraft since the wind direction is changing constantly within a very confined area. Cloud, called rotor or roll cloud, is often formed by this turbulent airflow. But the severe turbulence caused by the rotor is not always made visible by the presence of cloud.

The best way for pilots to avoid the danger zones associated with air flow over hills and mountains, is to avoid flying downwind of a range of mountains or hills, especially below the ridge line.

If it is necessary to fly over a mountain, pilots must do so with adequate separation from the crest or peak in order to avoid rotor turbulence in the lee of the mountain. Mountain waves will be present at the higher altitude, even though the cloud signs may not be there, but rotor cloud should not be encountered.

Significant lift can be experienced in the up-going part of mountain wave oscillations, especially forward of the leading edge of lenticular cloud. Glider pilots are able to soar to great altitude by exploiting the lift associated with mountain waves, which is propagated far up into the Stratosphere. The world glider altitude record stands at around 49 000 feet. The greatest altitude attained by a glider in soaring flight in Britain is over 31 000 feet. This record was gained over the Black Mountains in Wales where the highest peak is below 3 000 feet.

When planning a flight over mountainous terrain, gather as much preflight information as possible on cloud reports, wind direction, wind speed, and stability of air. Satellites often help locate mountain waves. Figures 84 and 85 are photographs of mountain wave clouds taken from spacecraft. Adequate information may not always be available, so remain alert for signposts in the sky. What should you look for both during preflight planning and during your inflight observations?

Wind at mountain top level in excess of 25 knots suggests some turbulence. Wind in excess of 40 knots across a mountain barrier dictates caution. Stratified clouds mean stable air. Standing lenticular and/or rotor clouds suggest a mountain wave; expect turbulence many miles to the lee of mountains and relative smooth flight on the windward side. Convective clouds on the windward side of mountains mean unstable air; expect turbulence in close proximity to and on either side of the mountain.

When approaching mountains from the leeward side during strong winds, begin your climb well away from the mountains-100 miles in a mountain wave and 30 to 50 miles otherwise. Climb to an altitude 3,000 to 5,000 feet above mountain tops before attempting to cross. The best procedure is to approach a ridge at a 45° angle to enable a rapid retreat to calmer air. If unable to make good on your first attempt and you have higher altitude capabilities, you may back off and make another attempt at higher altitude. Sometimes you may have to choose between turning back or detouring the area.

Flying mountain passes and valleys is not a safe procedure during high winds. The mountains funnel the wind into passes and valleys thus increasing wind speed and intensifying turbulence. If winds at mountain top level are strong, go high, or go around.

Surface wind may be relatively calm in a valley surrounded by mountains when wind aloft is strong. If taking off in the valley, climb above mountain top level before leaving the valley. Maintain lateral clearance from the mountains sufficient to allow recovery if caught in a downdraft.

147

Storms

The thunderstorm is one of the most spectacular atmospheric circulations, and one that you must respect as a pilot. It can be bright, loud, violent, and dangerous in many ways. In some tropical regions, thunderstorms occur year-round. In midlatitudes, they develop most frequently in spring, summer, and fall. Arctic regions occasionally experience thunderstorms during summer.

For a thunderstorm to form, the air must have sufficient water vapor, an unstable lapse rate, and an initial upward boost (lifting) to start the storm process in motion. There are a number of trigger mechanisms within the atmosphere and on the Earth's surface, which will cause air to ascend and, under the conditions mentioned above, begin the vigorous convective activity, required to form cumulonimbus cloud.

Unequal surface heating is a trigger mechanism. As the surface of the Earth heats up unequally, air lying in contact with the warmer surfaces will begin to rise. This is called convection. Convection is one of the main triggers for thunderstorms, especially over land in summer.

In mountainous areas, the trigger for thunderstorms can be the forced ascent of air as it flows up the windward side of mountains and hills. This is called orographic uplift.

If two air masses move together, air will be forced to rise through convergence.

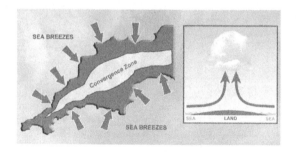

Air is also forced to rise by frontal uplift. Cumulonimbus thunder clouds are commonly associated with the vigorous uplift of air in advance of a cold front. But, very rarely, cumulonimbus may also be embedded in warm-front stratiform cloud, too.

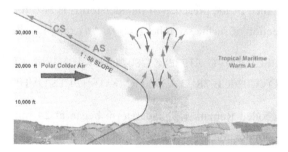

Based on surface observations, a thunderstorm is defined as a local storm produced by a cumulonimbus cloud, and always accompanied by lightning and thunder. It typically produces strong wind gusts, heavy rain, sometimes hail, and occasionally tornadoes. It is usually of short duration, rarely over two hours for a single storm. On the basis of flight experience, thunderstorms are also characterized by significant turbulence, icing, and wind shear.

Special (SPECI) weather observations are taken to mark the beginning and end of a thunderstorm, and to report significant changes in its intensity. Besides the standard coded information about sky condition, weather, visibility, pressure, temperature, and wind; evidence of the presence of thunderstorms is also found in the remarks section of surface weather reports. An example follows.

SPECI KCVG 312228Z 28024G36KT 3/4SM +TSRA SQ BKN008 OVC020CB 28/23 A3000 RMK TSB24 TS OVHD MOV E

Decoded Remarks: Thunderstorm began at 24 minutes past the hour. Thunderstorm is overhead moving east.

150

Thunderstorms Classification

There are two basic thunderstorm types: an ordinary thunderstorm, frequently described as an airmass thunderstorm, and a severe thunderstorm. A severe thunderstorm has a greater intensity than an airmass thunderstorm, as defined by the severity of the weather it produces: wind gusts of 50 knots or more and/or hail three-quarters of an inch or more in diameter and/or strong tornadoes.

The basic component of any thunderstorm is the cell. In the initial stages, this is the updraft region of the growing thunderstorm. Later in the thunderstorm development, it includes the precipitation-induced downdraft. A thunderstorm may exist as a single-cell, multicell, or supercell storm. A single-cell airmass thunderstorm lasts

151

less than one hour. In contrast, a supercell severe thunderstorm may last two hours or longer.

A multicell storm is a compact cluster of thunderstorms. It is usually composed of airmass thunderstorm cells and/or severe thunderstorm cells in different stages of development. These cells interact with each other to cause the duration of the cluster to be much longer than any individual cell.

The Life Cycle of Thunderstorms

There are three main stages in the development of a thunderstorm: the initial or cumulus stage, the mature, cumulonimbus stage and the dissipating stage.

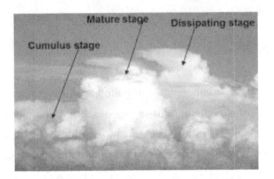

The three stages of the life cycle of a single-cell, airmass thunderstorm is illustrated bellow. Vertical dashed lines indicate boundaries of cool air descending with the rain shaft. Horizontal dashed lines indicate the freezing level.

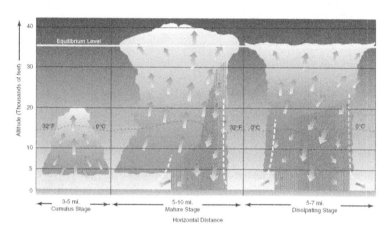

It is virtually impossible to visually detect the transition from one stage to another; the transition is subtle and by no means abrupt. Furthermore, a thunderstorm may be a cluster of cells in different stages of the life cycle.

The initial or cumulus stage: is characterized by strong updraughts and by the rapid growth, both horizontally and vertically, of a cumulus cloud. Strong updraughts produce clouds of great vertical extent, as air is drawn into the cloud from beneath and from the sides.

153

This initial stage usually lasts for around 20 minutes can produce a cloud up to 5 nm across and 25.000 ft high. The rapidly developing cumulus is often called cumulus congestus or towering cumulus. Early during the cumulus  stage, water droplets are quite small but grow to raindrop size as the cloud grows. The upwelling air carries the liquid water above the freezing level creating an icing hazard. As the raindrops grow still heavier, they fall. The cold rain drags air with it creating a cold downdraft coexisting with the updraft; the cell has reached the mature stage.

The mature stage: Precipitation beginning to fall from the cloud base is your signal that a downdraft has developed and a cell has entered the mature stage. Cold rain in the downdraft retards compressional heating, and the downdraft remains cooler than surrounding air. Therefore, its downward speed is accelerated and may exceed 2,500 feet per minute. The downrushing air spreads outward at the surface producing strong, gusty surface winds, a sharp temperature drop, and a rapid rise in pressure. The surface wind surge is a "plow wind" and its leading edge is the "first gust."

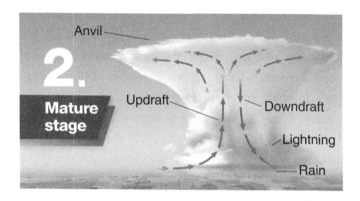

Meanwhile, updrafts reach a maximum with speeds possibly exceeding 6,000 feet per minute. Updrafts and downdrafts in close proximity create strong vertical shear and a very turbulent environment. All thunderstorm hazards reach their greatest intensity during the mature stage.

The rising and falling particles of rain, hail and snow cause a build up of static electricity within the cumulonimbus. The top of the cumulonimbus becomes positively charged while the lower part negatively charged. The negative charge at the base of the cumulonimbus induces a net positive charge on the Earth's surface beneath the cloud base.

The top of the mature cell often reaches into the lower stratosphere. The cumulonimbus cloud which is characteristic of this stage is easily identified by the appearance of its top. The highest portion of the cloud develops a cirruform appearance because of the very cold temperatures and the strong stability of the stratosphere. Vertical motions are dampened and the cloud spreads out horizontally, finally forming the well-known anvil shape. When the anvil top forms, it points in the direction of the winds at the top of the thunderstorm. This is approximately the direction that the storm is moving.

156

In high-based storms, lightning and thunder occur, but the precipitation often evaporates before reaching the ground. In this case, only a veil of precipitation known as VIRGA is observed immediately below the cloud base. The combination of lightning and gusty winds in the absence of precipitation is often a cause of forest fires. Also, despite the lack of rain, the associated downdraft and gusty winds can still produce flight hazards such as strong downdrafts and turbulence.

The dissipating stage: The dissipating stage of a cumulonimbus thunder cloud, begins as the anvil top becomes fully formed. The dissipating stage is characterized predominately by downdraughts. However, updraughts may still prevail at the summit of the cumulonimbus, feeding the growing anvil. Precipitation at this stage is usually heavy, but more widespread and less intense than at the mature stage.

Precipitation and downdrafts spread throughout the lower levels of the thunderstorm cell, cutting off the updraft. Since the source of energy for thunderstorm growth is the supply of heat and moisture from the surface layer, the cutoff of the updraft spells the end of the storm.

With no source of moisture, the precipitation decreases and the entire thunderstorm cloud takes on a stratiform appearance, gradually dissipating. Because the anvil top is an ice cloud, it often lasts longer than the rest of the cell. Although the typical lifetime of a single-cell airmass thunderstorm is less than an hour, odds are that you have encountered thunderstorms that have lasted much longer. How can this be? In such cases, the explanation is that you were actually observing a multicell thunderstorm or a supercell thunderstorm, both of which last longer and affect larger areas than an airmass thunderstorm.

The dissipating stage may last for between 1 1/2 and 2 1/2 hours, during which time, lightning and thunder may continue to occur. Isolated thunderstorms, although on occasions quite large, do not last long, because the severe downdraughts which accompany the precipitation suppress the up-currents necessary to sustain the cloud. Isolated thunderstorms, then, effectively begin to dissipate once precipitation commences.

Chapter 4

Operations

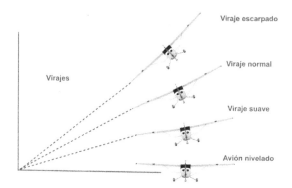

Straight and Level Flight

Once you reach the final 1000 feet, it's time to start our first straight and level flight. This is the first maneuver that we should learn on our way to becoming PP since it will be essential to keep the plane with level wings, a constant speed and without gaining or losing height. For this purpose, we will begin to experience the sensations that the plane can generate for us, feel when it "falls", feel when it "gets up", feel its acceleration or slowdown. Each of these sensations will be incorporated into each of you as you spend the flight hours on the plane, so don't despair!

One of the most used techniques for straight and level flight is to take as a visual reference "the horizon line" to determine if we are climbing, descending or turning the wings to one side or the other. Let's look at the following example to understand how this visual reference would be official.

Straight and Level Aircraft: Let's consider the broken line in the following graph as the horizon line. Let's see how the front panel of the plane is located just above the horizon line and the wings of the plane located parallel to it.

163

Let's see below how the horizon line should be seen with respect to the plane panel but from inside the cabin.

It could be very helpful to take a reference inside the cabin, for example, taking the "Compass" as a reference and considering the level plane when it is right on the horizon line.

Having this reference, we will know when the plane has a tendency to descend if the compass is below the horizon line and a tendency to ascend if the compass is above it.

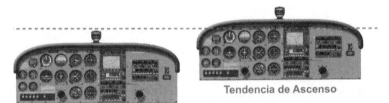

Tendencia de Descenso

Tendencia de Ascenso

Turns

Once the Straight and Level Flight is mastered, it's time for turns, commonly known as "Spins." Based on a simple theoretical concept, turns are the voluntary tendency of the plane to tilt the plane (wing) to the side in order to generate a turn. However, that inclination can be of a certain number of degrees with respect to the transverse axis of the plane in a straight and level flight. According to the number of degrees adopted by each inclination, each turn will be classified with a specific name, being:

Smooth Turn: 15° inclination.

Normal Turn: 30° inclination.

Steep Turn: 45° inclination.

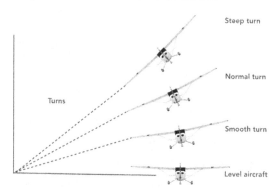

Let's see how the horizon line should be seen in each turn from inside the cockpit:

Smooth Turn:

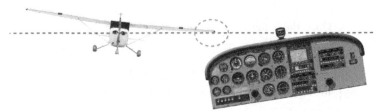

We take as a reference the Horizon line and tilting the plane until the wing tip "touches" Imaginarily to the line, as seen in the figure on the left (outside view). In turn, from the inside, we see that the edge of the panel rests just above the horizon line.

Normal Turn:

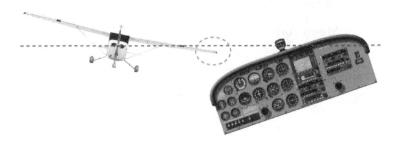

We take as a reference the horizon line and tilting the plane until the tip of the wing imaginary "Pass" below of the line, as seen in the figure on the left (outside view). In turn, from the inside, we see that the edge of the panel exceeds the horizon line, being above it.

Steep Turn:

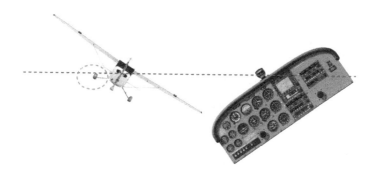

We take the horizon line as a reference and tilt the plane until the wheel of the main train "Touches" imaginarily to the line, as seen in the figure on the left (outside view). In turn, from the inside, we see that the edge of the panel exceeds the horizon line, being well above

"S" on a road

The purpose of this maneuver is the practice of turns and "Distributive Attention", seeking control of the aircraft and its height and speed parameters but in turn controlling the distance to the external visual reference. The maneuver is based on making "S" on a straight reference, flying over it perpendicularly and once past it, making a 180° turn to fly over the reference again, this will "imaginarily" draw a semicircle on the chosen path and later when flying over it over the second time, we will make another turn on the other side of 180°. In this way, the route of the plane will form "S" on the chosen reference, as shown in the following graph:

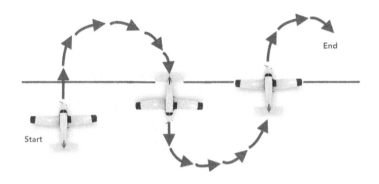

Turn Around a Point

This maneuver is intended to exercise 360° turns at a constant radius on a visual reference. This practice will help the pilot fly the plane without losing visual references of its exterior, maintaining the same distance from the reference and without modifying the height. The maneuver begins with "tail wind" and consists of taking a visual reference to make a turn around it, maintaining a constant radius of distance and without gaining or losing height. Start once the plane is parallel to the chosen reference. From there, a gentle turn begins (in principle) without losing sight of the reference. The effect of the wind must be considered to always maintain a constant radius to the reference and the initial height of the maneuver.

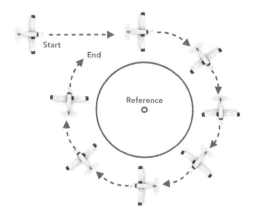

"8" Around a Point

Arriving at more advanced and more precise maneuvers, it's time to make "eight" around two points or visual references (trees, houses, etc.). The objective of this maneuver will be to train the Pilot in 360° turns to one side and the other without stopping, adding the obligation to maintain a constant radius to each reference and managing to fly level at the chosen height, without gaining or losing height or speed.

Although, it seems simple, it is not at all, since it keeps certain complexities in terms of the need to keep adequate "Distributive Attention" constant about the flight parameters of the plane and the chosen visual references. Let's look at the following graph to understand what it is and then we will develop the procedure:

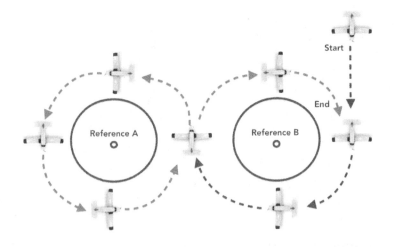

As we can see in the graph above, the procedure begins next to the references. Once placed lateral to the first reference, we started in the same way as we would in a "Turn Around a Point", rest the tip of the wing on reference A and start a smooth turn around it, maintaining a constant radius and level height. We will continue this first step until we move "Lateral" to the two references together.

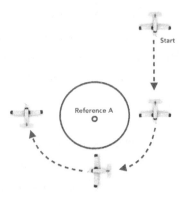

In this second step, we must make a complete turn around the second reference (B) until we cross sides again to the two points, as shown in the figure below:

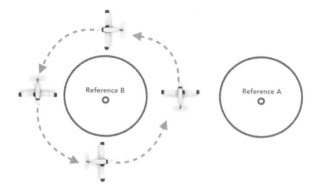

For the third and last step we must cross both references sideways and start a turn around point A, keeping the radius and height constant. The exercise will end when moving sideways to reference A, the starting point of the maneuver, as we see in this last graphic example:

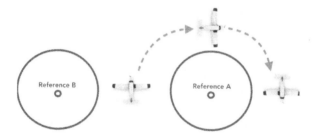

Summarizing: Start laterally to reference A, make a 180° rotation around it until you go sideways to the two references (A and B). When moving sideways to both references, make a complete 360° rotation around reference B, until moving sideways to both references again. Finally, when passing, again, sideways to both

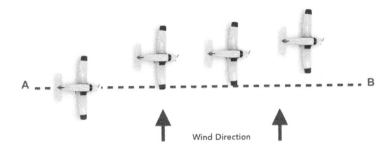

Wind Direction

Drift Correction

When flying on a straight and level flight, there are external factors that tend to move us away from our flight path, moving to one side or the other and generating a deviation or "Drift" from our route. Wind is usually the main influential factor in this kind of deviation, so a procedure called "Drift Correction" comes into play. This procedure will help compensate for such deviation and keep our plane on the desired route or trajectory. Let's see an example:

As we can see in the graph, the desired flight path from point A to point B is affected by the deviation or drift generated by the force of the wind which pushes the plane to one side of the route, leaving it completely out of it.

The "Drift Correction" try to avoid this unwanted displacement, correcting the course of the planned route and facing the nose of the plane towards the direction from which the wind

172

comes. This would generate a force that subtracts the drift by the action of the wind. Let's see an example:

Wind Direction

Analyzing the graph, we see how when facing the nose with the wind, it generates a force that prevents an unwanted displacement of our route. As a result, the plane will find itself flying a trajectory from point A to point B, with a different course from that of the planned trajectory but we will consider this difference, not as an error but as a correction and we will give it the name of "Drift Correction".

From the cabin of the plane, we will notice this correction taking a visual point of reference right in front of us and on the desired trajectory. After applying the "Drift Correction" the reference point should be in the same place along the flown section although with a slight deviation from the initial course.

Incorporation into the Traffic Pattern

Once the height of the traffic pattern has been reached (let's suppose 700 feet by way of example), it's time to join it.

Like every step we take in aviation, we will do it with a specific procedure so that all aircraft enter the transit pattern in the same way, thus avoiding incidents or accidents.

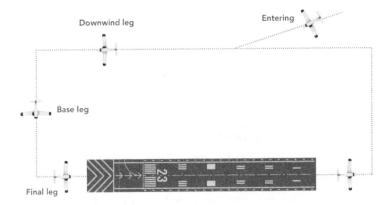

We will start from incorporation, seeking to enter the "initial" section parallel to the runway and in the opposite direction to landing. The right sector to join "Initial" is right side to the opposite track. Once we manage to reach this position, we will continue with the normal transit circuit, passing through its following sections: "downwind" section, "Base" section and "Final" section. The configuration of the aircraft will depend on the type of approach to be developed.

Approach Procedures

When we refer to an approach procedure, we talk about a logical sequence of configuration of the aircraft and management of its resources. The real objective of this procedure is to take the plane to the "End" section of the circuit, prior to landing, and reach it in the safest configuration, having controlled the parameters of "Speed, Height, Heading and Power". This is where two new terms introduced to Private Plane Pilots come into play, we will talk about "Stabilized" and "Unstabilized" approaches. While these terms are not a requirement of the aeronautical authority to obtain the PP license, they are undoubtedly new and extremely important concepts for the safe operation of a flight, either for a PP or for an Airline Pilot.

90° Approach

Let's start with the most used approach for a normal flight. It takes place during a normal traffic circuit and respecting its three sections (initial-basic-final). For this purpose, we must define the parameters we want to obtain for each section, that is, a height and speed defined for the initial section, the same for the basic section and the same for the final section. These parameters could vary depending on the plane to be flown and/or operating criteria of the person flying it. Let's take the following parameters "only" as an example:

- ✓ **Downwing: 700 FT 80 KT**
- ✓ **Base: 600 FT 75 KT**
- ✓ **Final: 500 FT 70 KT**

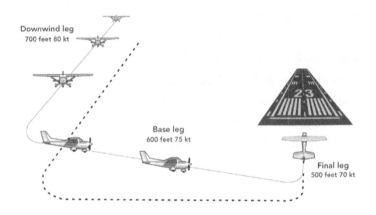

Analyzing the graph, we can observe the parameters defined for each section. We started by entering the transit circuit in the initial size and looking to reach 700 feet and 80 knots of speed. We continue flying in the opposite direction to the landing until we move sideways to the runway in use. From there we continue flying for 30 more seconds to get away from the track and ensure that the basic section has a good and comfortable distance to it.

176

180° Approach

Before detailing this procedure, let's understand its purpose and importance. Unlike the 90-degree approach, in which we perform the entire procedure with the help of engine power; in this 180-degree approach, the power only intervenes in the initial section, since the rest of the procedure until landing, must be done with reduced power, or as they say, in glide. One of the main advantages of performing this procedure is the practice of gliding flight during a 180-degree turn, downhill and without the help of power. Let's analyze the following graph:

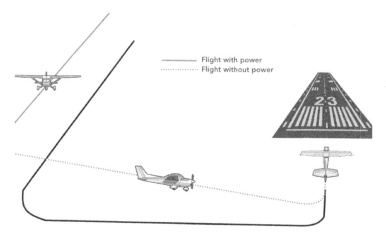

360° Approach

As in the previous case, let's first understand the purpose of practicing a 360° approach. In the same way as the 180° approach, the complete procedure should be performed on a flight without power or as it is said "Planning".

The objective of this practice will be to instruct the Pilot to a flight without power, making a 360° descent turn and configuring the plane for landing. Without a doubt, one of the most precise and demanding maneuvers of the PP course so it is usually taught at an advanced stage of the course, where the Pilot already knows the plane and its different behaviors. Understanding the requirement and precision required for the practice of this approach, it is highly advisable not to try to practice it at the beginning of the PPA course, since at that initial stage priority should be given to knowing the plane on a flight with maneuvers of less complexity, to then move slowly and add difficulty to the maneuvers as the Pilot progresses.

Differentiating it from the rest of the approaches, this approach will begin just above the track, at a height of 1000 feet. It will start once the aircraft is flying above the runway numbers, and in the same direction as landing, and then start a complete 360-degree turn, but divided into 3 stages that we will study below. Let's analyze the graph and see the steps to follow and, by way of example, suppose that the runway is "23", that is, the final landing course will be 230°

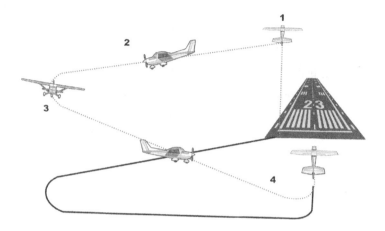

1) Fly over the start of the runway, with a height of 1000 FT and in the same direction as landing (route 230°).

2) Total power reduction and start the first turn of 135° (toward heading 095°), down and to the side of the traffic circuit. At this stage it is suggested to be able to descend 300 FT, to reach the next stage with 700 FT. Just before starting stage 3, perform an "engine cleaning", giving soft but progressive power and then reduce it again.

3) Continue with the second turn also of 135° (towards course 320°), in descent similar to the Basic section of a normal circuit. At this stage it is suggested to descend 200 FT, to reach the next one with 500 FT. Just before starting the stage

179

4, perform an "engine cleaning", giving power smoothly but progressively and then reduce it again.

4) Finally, when reaching 500 feet, start the last turn, this time 90°, towards the final approach with 500 FT and the track right in front, as would be done on a normal circuit, but with the exception that we will continue in glide and without power in the engine.

For a better assimilation of the steps, let's see how it would look from a plan view from above:

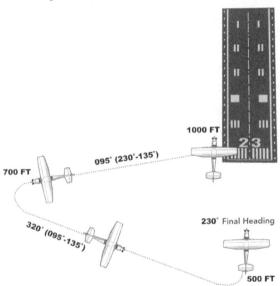

Normal landing

Landing is the most critical phase of the flight for any aircraft, whatever its size and / or configuration. When we talk about a landing, we talk about a critical but controlled maneuver. Landings are usually, always and each of them, completely different from each other. The particularity of this maneuver makes it a unique and unrepeatable situation, but always carried out with the same procedure by the flight crew.

Let's think of landing as a controlled and intentional stall maneuver, since its essence lies precisely in that: "Lose controlled and intentionally sustain until you gently touch the floor of the runway."

Now, let's divide 3 parts when landing to study it in more detail:

1) Before contact with the ground (in the air).
2) During contact with the ground (in the air / on the ground).
3) After making contact with the ground (on land).

1) The appropriate power must be maintained to keep the speed constant, since we will be flying at very low speed and very close to losing lift. You must continue flying with this configuration (level wings and minimum speed) until you go through the start of the track

at 50 FT, where we should completely cut the engine power and move on to the next stage.

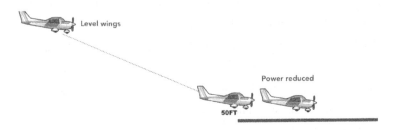

2) Once the engine power is cut, the plane's trend will be to maintain your flight path, so it will continue to head to the ground. For this reason, this is where the famous and well-known "FLARE" or recovered comes into play.

The "Flare" consists of acting on the deep rudder of the plane, carrying back the control command very smoothly and with the intention of slightly raising the nose of the plane. With this action, the plane should cut its downward trend, changing its attitude and taking a flight parallel to the runway. As the speed continues to decrease, the plane will descend until it touches the ground at low speed and parallel to it.

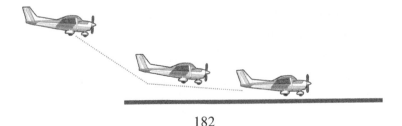

A wrong "Flare" could lead to an unwanted situation, let's see:

Too high a "Flare" would cause the plane to fly parallel to the runway with excessive height and when running out of speed, it goes into "loss" and collapse falling sharply to the ground.

On the other hand, a "Flare" too low, would cause the plane to hit the ground hard with the descent attitude it had previously, since there was not enough time for the plane to raise its nose and change the attitude.

Once the correct "Flare" has been made, we touch the floor of the track and continue with the next stage.

3) After making a correct "Flare" and making contact with the runway, the plane will be rolling at high speed. In this situation it is recommended to pay special care to the manipulation of the "Pedals" to control the taxiing, since at high speeds, excessive

pressure on the control surface could cause unwanted movement, taking the plane to one side of the runway edge.

The correct procedure will be to make contact with the runway, control the plane by gently exerting pressure on the pedals to keep it on the runway axis during the "landing run" until the plane slows down and allows brakes to be applied to completely stop its gear.

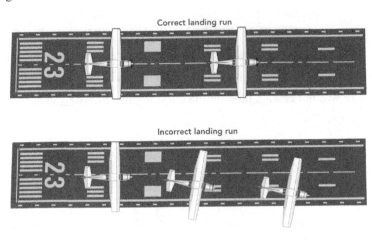

Crosswind Landing

Once the concept of a normal landing has been assimilated, it is time to add a typical complication that usually occurs in most landings. During a normal landing with calm wind, when adopting the final runway course we should reach it with the plane centered on its axis and land without major inconvenience. But the situation changes when unfavorable wind conditions arise from one side of our landing path. This situation tends to generate a displacement of the plane in the direction of the wind, running us to the side of the landing path. Let's see:

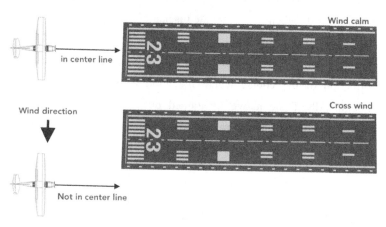

There are several techniques for a landing with crosswind. They tend to guarantee a correct approach, and a centered landing on the axis of the runway. Wrongly, it is usually believed that it should land as in conditions of calm wind, that is, go through the start of the runway and completely reduce the power, or go through the start of the runway with the power already reduced previously. This is a mistake. The lack of power in the engine will leave the plane more vulnerable to speed changes, due to the effect of the blow of the wind on the fuselage. Therefore, one of the recommended techniques is to approach and land with power until the moment of performing the Flare. This will ensure that you have the necessary power to compensate for the possible variation in speed.

Another commonly used technique is the action of "Lower or Tilt" slightly the wing on the side where the wind comes from. This action will cause an aerodynamic force with a tendency to turn to that side, against subtracting the displacement force that the wind could generate when impacting the fuselage.

Normally, an approximation with applied power and a slight correction of the course where the wind comes from is usually enough. All of the above mentioned during the final stretch of landing should be enough to counteract the deviation that the side wind could generate if corrective action is not taken.

Missed Approach or Go Around

Reaching the end of the instruction in this manual, it is the turn of an indispensable procedure to avoid an incident or accident. We will talk about the "missed Approach" or commonly called "go around".

Basically, it is a procedure by which the landing will be aborted, applying all the power to the engine and seeking to ascend again to the height of the traffic circuit to start a new approach.

The "go around" is commonly performed during the final approach and before touching the track. The reasons why we should make an "Escape" can be many and all will be valid if you cooperate to avoid an incident. Let's detail the most common factors that usually end in an "Escape":

- "Unstabilized" approach below 200 FT.
- Total or partial lack of control of the plane.
- Occupied runway.
- Adverse weather conditions.
- Runway incursion by another aircraft.
- Calculation error.
- Discomfort on the part of the Pilot.
- And any other factor that the Pilot decides would be better to make a new approach! All Valid!

To develop the procedure, we have to consider that when applying all the power of the engine, the plane will abruptly change its attitude, so it is recommended to maintain the runway axis until it exceeds 500 FT and thus achieve a safe height without excessive maneuvers. The procedure is very simple and consists of 4 simple steps:

1) Make the decision!
2) Apply all the power, controlling the plane.
3) Start ascent by keeping the track axis up to 500 FT.
4) After 300 FT, reduce the power to ascent configuration and continue with it up to 500 FT. Then proceed as planned.

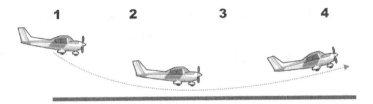

Use of Flaps during landing

As in the takeoff stage, high lift devices such as Flaps are very important in the landing phase. Its operating principle during this stage is based on allowing the aircraft to fly at a lower speed, allowing it, among other things, to increase its downhill slope without increasing its speed too much. Another benefit of using the Flaps on landing will be the reduction of the approach and touch speed in order to use a smaller portion of the runway when landing, usually used in landings for short fields or with obstacles in the glide path. Let's see some examples:

Imagine a descent slope where the final approach is interrupted by an obstacle, in this case, trees on the edge of the runway. A fairly common situation on rural runways or aerodromes with parks and / or forests near the runway.

Landing with obstacles

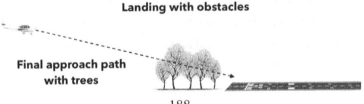

Final approach path with trees

Faced with this scenario, the aircraft could not comply with a normal approach path, since it would be in the direction of collision with the obstacle. The aircraft has two possible paths to land on the desired runway managing to overcome the obstacle. You can change the height of your final approach and maintain the descent path planned with the appropriate speed for such a maneuver, then perform the Flare, and finally the landing run, as we have seen in previous pages. Taking this option there is a risk that the runway length will not be long enough for the aircraft to be able to perform all these maneuvers safely.

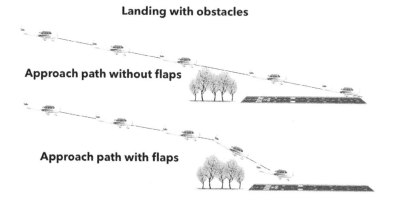

Landing with obstacles

Approach path without flaps

Approach path with flaps

The other option is to operate a steeper descent to FULL FLAPS, allowing the aircraft to increase its descent rate without considerably increasing the speed. By increasing your descent rate, you will find the runway at a much shorter distance than in the previous example, which will allow you to perform the Flare and continue with the landing run with a runway available.

189

Now let's imagine another example. Let's look at the following obstacle-free approach but on a short runway or field, or at least shorter than usual. Here the same operating principle is fulfilled as in the previous example. The ultimate goal will be to land and brake at the shortest possible runway distance.

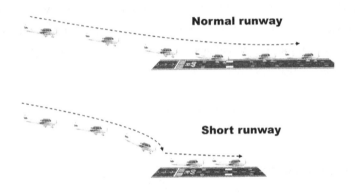

To achieve the goal, it will be necessary to approach at a lower speed than usual for a normal runway. We know that extending the Flaps delays the Vs, therefore, the aircraft could fly at a lower speed without reaching the stall. This will allow the aircraft to perform a much shorter braking run than usual. On the other hand, if the height of the final approach is high, the aircraft will need to increase its descent regime but without increasing the speed to respect the previous principle. When operating the aircraft with full Flaps it will be possible to increase the descent regime without increasing the speed. To understand this concept, let's analyze the lifting formula.

190

Recalling the lifting formula, we find two modifiable variables: speed and wing surface.

$$L = CL \cdot \tfrac{1}{2}\,\rho \cdot S \cdot V^2$$

As an example, we are going to give a numerical value to each of these variables to understand the previous example.

$$L = CL \cdot \tfrac{1}{2}\,\rho \cdot S \cdot V^2$$
$$L = CL \cdot \tfrac{1}{2}\,\rho \cdot 10 \cdot 20$$

In order to keep the lifting value constant, the surface has a value of 10 and the speed a value of 20. By increasing the area to a value of 15, we can reduce the speed to a value of 15 and keep the lift value constant. In other words, by increasing the surface we can delay the stall speed, the effect of high lift devices.

- What do you think would happen if we increased the wing surface without slowing down?

If your answer was "Increased lift", you are right. When modifying one of the variables of the lift formula, we must compensate by modifying another variable to keep the initial value constant, otherwise there will be a change in that value.

Made in the USA
Las Vegas, NV
17 October 2024

97039953R00108